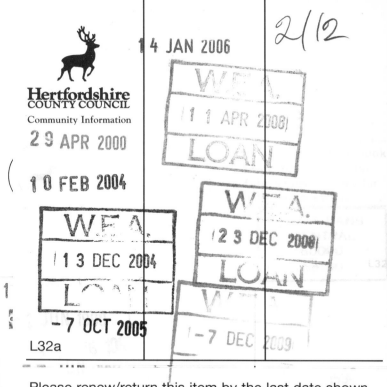

2/12

14 JAN 2006

**Hertfordshire**
COUNTY COUNCIL

Community Information

2 9 APR 2000

1 0 FEB 2004

W.E.A.

1 1 APR 2008

LOAN

W.E.A.

1 3 DEC 2004

LOAN

W.E.A.

2 3 DEC 2008

LOAN

− 7 OCT 2005

− 7 DEC 2009

L32a

---

Please renew/return this item by the last date shown.

So that your telephone call is charged at local rate, please call the numbers as set out below:

|  | From Area codes 01923 or 0208: | From the rest of Herts: |
|---|---|---|
| Renewals: | 01923 471373 | 01438 737373 |
| Enquiries: | 01923 471333 | 01438 737333 |
| Minicom: | 01923 471599 | 01438 737599 |

L32b

# THE MEDES AND PERSIANS

CASSELL'S EARLY CULTURE SERIES
*Series Editor: Edward R. Sammis*

*Historical Adviser: T. Cuyler Young, Jr.*
Curator, Iranian Antiquities, Royal Ontario Museum, Toronto, Canada

# The MEDES and PERSIANS

*Conquerors and Diplomats*

Robert Collins

*Illustrated in black and white and full colour*

CASSELL · LONDON

For my parents,
Floy and Jack Collins

CASSELL & COMPANY LTD
35 Red Lion Square, London WC1R 4SG
Sydney, Auckland, Toronto, Johannesburg

First published in Great Britain 1974

ISBN 0 304 29270 2

Art secured by McGraw-Hill and Fratelli Fabbri and reproduced by
agreement with Fratelli Fabbri. Editor: Marie Shaw; Art and Design:
James K. Davis and Barbara Rasmussen

Printed in Italy by Fratelli Fabbri Editori, Milano, and bound in Great
Britain

F 673

# Contents

An excavated site north of Istakhr in Iran where archaeologists from the
Oriental Institute have been working.

# Introduction

ARCHAEOLOGICAL discoveries in the past generation have enhanced greatly our knowledge of the ancient Medes and Persians, our relatives of long ago. The glories of Persepolis and Pasargadae, the home capitals of the Persian kings, now stand revealed to us in a grandeur that staggers the imagination. Excavations in progress are shedding new light on the Medes and on the very origins of Iranian civilization.

Until now most of our books on the Medes and Persians told their tale in terms of spectacular battles and protracted wars, and were usually written from a Greek point of view. Hence the Medes and the Persians often got rather short shrift. In consequence the student in the west has been taught to look upon the Greeks as the glorious defenders of his cultural heritage in their wars with the Achaemenid Empire. Had there been no gallant Spartan stand at Thermopylae, no Athenian-led victory at Marathon and Salamis, no allied Greek triumph at Plataea, civilization would have been still-born—or so these ancient stories would have us believe. The independent, vigorous, cultured, democratic Greeks would have fallen under the heel of oriental despotism; youthful Europe would have lapsed into barbarism. This has been the traditional version of the story in the west since the fifth century B.C.

Yet from an Iranian viewpoint these celebrated conflicts were probably little more than border incidents, scarcely affecting the onward march of mighty imperial affairs. And as for civilization versus barbarism, an Iranian would have had rather different opinions on that!

It is time then for the west to be more widely exposed to an objective account of the exploits and contributions of the Medes and the Persians—of their achievements and their failures, their religion, customs, ways of life in peace as well as in war, and their contribution to civilization in the broadest sense. Who were the Iranians, where did they come from, what was the genius that allowed them to found, almost overnight, an empire on so grand a scale? What gave their art and culture a civilizing life and vigor which has survived both in their ancient monuments and in the traditions of modern Iran?

Today we live in a shrinking world. As more frequent and persistent contact develops between us and the non-western world, we are constantly disturbed by how difficult it is to communicate with other cultures and other traditions. One way to ease our frustrations with these difficulties is to keep in mind that there are two sides to every story. We need to read the histories of other cultures at best through their eyes, at a minimum through neutral eyes.

Alexander, barbarian though he may have been to both Greeks and Iranians, had a dream when he set out to conquer the by then politically decadent empire of the Persians. In a rather crude and naive Macedonian way he wanted to Hellenize the east, to bring to it the civilization of Greece which he himself had adopted. He did not live to carry out this program, and without his energy and vision, it failed. But he lived long enough to glimpse the truth that in a real meeting of east and west it was by no means clear who was going to be teacher and who student, who was civilized and who was barbarian. Read the story which follows with this thought in mind.

*T. Cuyler Young, Jr.*
*Curator, West Asian Department*
*Royal Ontario Museum*

chapter 1

THE MAN WHO BUILT A BETTER ARMY

HE was a swarthy ruffian in sheepskin coat and high laced boots—hardly the kind of romantic and elegant figure that we now associate with the word *king*. But to his people in that year of 625 B.C., Cyaxares, king of the Medes, was as noble a monarch as ever lived.

He ruled a mountainous kingdom of perhaps 14,000 square miles in the western part of what is now the Iranian plateau, south of the Black and Caspian seas. For generation after generation his people had been harassed by the Assyrians, a more highly developed people who reigned supreme in that part of the ancient world. But Cyaxares finally had had enough. He was tired of being bullied. He set out to crush his subjects' tormentors, and—although he never dreamed of this—he set world history on a new path.

His Iranian name was Uvakhshatra, but we know him by the easier, westernized version, Cyaxares. History left no pictures of him but we can reconstruct his appearance from the story of his life and his era. He was short; the entire human race was smaller in that seventh century before Christ. His naturally dark complexion was burned darker by sun and wind. His body was hard and sinewy from years in the saddle. His hands were calloused from a lifetime of grasping spear handles and rawhide reins.  Yet Cyaxares had more than physical strength.  He had a restless mind, and an idea that spawned an empire.

His was a small and immediate world, filled with perils.  To the north and east were roaming bandit tribes, among them the fearsome Scythians.  To the west were the powerful Assyrians and the smug, comfortable Babylonians.  It was world enough for a man to wrap his mind around in a time when it took an army two days to march as far as today's average commuter drives in an hour.

Perhaps from old men's tales around the campfires Cyaxares heard vague hints of his own origins, a smattering of what historians have since discovered: Long before his time waves of migrant people flowed from somewhere in central Asia (probably the Russian steppes) to what is now western Asia and Europe.  They spoke a common language, broken into many dialects, that became known as Aryan.  (The word *Aryan,* coming from the ancient Indian language Sanskrit, meant a man of good or noble family.)  Some went to Italy and Greece; some became the Celts (the Welsh, Irish, and Scots) of western Europe; others became Germans, Scandinavians, or Slavs.  For all these groups individual languages evolved.

And some of the wanderers — ancestors of Cyaxares — settled on the high land of the Iranian plateau ("land of the Aryans").  Here, in rough country between two great mountain ranges, the Zagros and Elburz, they separated into two fairly distinct peoples.  There were the Parsa and Parsumash (who became the Persians) and the Madai (later the Medes).  For a long time there was no

**Artist's drawing of battle shows Assyrians in action.**

real unity even within these divisions.   Each mountain valley had its tribe, ruled by a leader who lived in a tall, strongly fortified stone castle.   Finally they appeared in written history as identifiable units: the Persians in 844 B.C., the Medes in 836.

The Medes for the most part were probably nomadic herdsmen and hunters, small tough men with neat, curled beards and short hair tied back from their faces.   Their clothes were of cowhide and wool; their food was milk, mutton, and beef.   They sowed small plots of grain, reaped it with sickles, and baked unleavened bread.   They raced chariots; gambled with dice; sang and danced to the flute, lute, and drum; raided each other's herds; fought among themselves; and hunched their backs against the elements.   Nature made everyday survival difficult enough.   Now, more and more, the Assyrians were making life intolerable.

Assyria was a rich, old, complex civilization.   Compared to the nomads from the hills, the Assyrians were highly literate. They carved stone relief art, fashioned ornaments and utensils of bronze and gold, and even had libraries.   In 1849 British archaeologist Sir Henry Layard, in a dig at the site of Nineveh, the Assyrian capital, uncovered "two large chambers of which the whole area was piled a foot or more deep in tablets."   In other similar discoveries some twenty-five thousand clay tablets were recovered for the British Museum.   These were literary, religious, scientific, and business documents.

The Assyrians, however, were no mere peaceable seekers of knowledge.   They also maintained a splendid army.   It was a masterpiece of organization: cavalry; light infantry (bowmen and slingers); heavy infantry (lancers); and a corps of engineers who dug trenches under enemy walls, threw earthen bridges across moats, and smashed gates with huge battering rams.

Whenever fancy struck them, they marched into the Zagros to take "gifts" from the Medes and Persians — particularly the fine Nesaean horses.   Cyaxares' father, Khshathrita, had died fighting the Assyrians.   Now Cyaxares vowed he would avenge all his people.   But first he would have to build a better army.

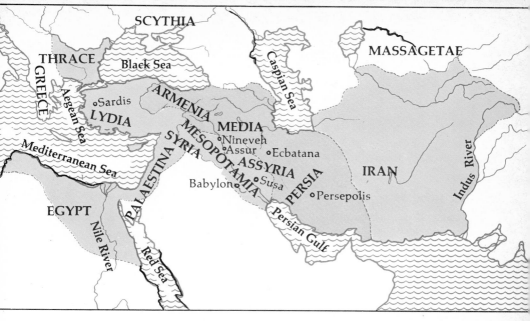

**The Persian Empire**

The Kingdom of the Medes
The Persian Empire

His mountain Medes were as brave as any other people. They were superb, daring horsemen on their fast, sturdy little mounts, and they possessed strengths and skills acquired from a lifetime on breakneck mountain trails. They were hardier than the Assyrians; anyone who had eked out a living in the hills and survived winter temperatures well below freezing *had* to be tough.

But their spears and rectangular wicker shields and their jumbled rushing attacks had proved no match for the well-drilled Assyrian army and its deadly archers, in particular. The Medes needed better weapons and better fighting tactics.

Cyaxares came up with a technique that his descendants would use over and over again to build an empire. He studied his enemies' strategy, then took their best idea and improved upon it: in this case the way in which his foe's army was organized.

First he set about training squads of his best men in the art of the bow and arrow, getting some coaching from the Scythians. By then he had pacified those bandit tribes, who for decades had darted in and out of other people's territory, looting and pillaging. For twenty-eight years before Cyaxares came to the throne, they had held much of Media.   One story has it that Cyaxares invited the Scythian chieftains to a friendly dinner, plied them with wine, and when they were nodding over their cups, had them all killed on the spot.   It probably wasn't that simple, but by 625 B.C. he had won back his kingdom.   The Scythians, now more or less subservient, showed themselves to be expert advisers on archery.

To this new skill Cyaxares added an Assyrian touch: the organization of his entire army into archers, spearmen, and cavalry. He turned the cavalry into a lethal striking-force, able to sweep in on an enemy at full gallop, firing arrows with deadly accuracy. Then they would wheel away before the enemy could recover.

At last he was ready to try his new army against his neighbors, the Persians.  He promptly crushed them.  But with another bit of wisdom that his descendants would also adopt, he allowed the Persians to retain their own government.  It was an easy way to keep subjected people satisfied and peaceful.

Then, in the year 615 B.C., Cyaxares moved out from Ecbatana (now buried under the modern city of Hamadan in Iran), his lofty capital located 6,280 feet above sea level.  He turned his back on the mud-brick battlements of the city, on the passes still white with traces of winter snow, on the rushing mountain streams, on the flocks of sheep and goats, and rode down toward Assyria and his long-awaited revenge.

The city of Arrapkha fell before him.  He marched on toward Nineveh, where his father had died in battle.  Proud old Nineveh, on the Tigris River in what is now Iraq, sprawled over 1,850

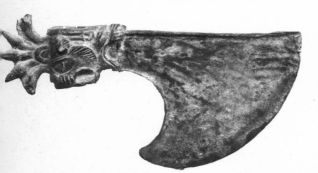

This heavy, bronze axe was a formidable weapon. British Museum.

acres surrounded by eight miles of thick mud-brick walls faced with stone, in which were set eighteen large gates. Eighteen canals sucked water down from neighboring hills. Inside towered a palace with eighty rooms, many of them lined with statuary and friezes. Nineveh was a tempting prize, but too invincible for Cyaxares — as yet.

He made one attempt to gain entry but was unsuccessful. He camped for a while outside the walls, then withdrew his forces, resolving to come back another day with greater strength.

By the autumn of 614 he was battering Ashur, Assyria's second largest city, south of Nineveh on the Tigris. There his Medes smashed through the thin limestone walls without difficulty. They leveled buildings, slaughtered most of the men, and carried off the women — standard procedure in wars of that day. Then Cyaxares went home to rest and to perfect more plans.

Already he had made history, having laid the cornerstone of what one day would be known as the Achaemenid Empire of the ancient Medes and Persians. Soon after Cyaxares' time it would become the greatest empire the world had ever known. Superimposed on a map today, it would sprawl across Turkey, Syria, Israel, Egypt, Libya, Iraq, Iran, Afghanistan, much of Pakistan, a bit of Bulgaria, Greece, and European Russia, and large sections of Soviet Turkmen.

The Achaemenid Empire lasted only three centuries, but its impact rolled on through the ages. It gave us some of mankind's richest history. From those days come marching the heroes and villains of the Old Testament. There was Daniel in the lions' den; wicked King Nebuchadrezzar (who appears in the Bible as Nebuchadnezzar) of Babylon; rich King Croesus of Lydia — all reminding us that the Bible is a historical document, although not always strictly accurate. Achaemenid times gave us other ringing romantic names: Leonidas and his Spartans holding the pass at Thermopylae; Alexander the Great; the Hanging Gardens of Babylon (one of the seven wonders of the ancient world); the battle of Marathon and the "marathon run." Wars, plots, intrigues, real, yet exciting as fiction — all of these made up the world of the Medes and Persians.

The Achaemenid rulers were no saints. At worst they were cold-blooded tyrants. But the best of them, although as ruthless as necessary to gain power, helped move mankind a little farther up the ladder of civilization.

(Below.) Graceful bronze is typical of Elamite art. (Right) Two figures of worshippers present offering of lamb. Statuette at top is made of silver; bottom, of gold alloy. Louvre.

They did it as did Cyaxares in his gentler moments: by absorbing, adapting, improving on the best of other cultures; by practicing a sort of creative management of their subjects. Often they let captive countries keep their own customs, religion, forms of administration, even local officials — all of which, woven together, made a stronger empire. (There was little incentive for rebellion when most of the ruling officials were neighbors.)

In three centuries of empire they adopted a religion, Zoroastrianism, that has been described as "the least pagan in a pagan world." In it we find some roots of Judaism and Christianity, particularly an ethical relationship between God and man and an emphasis on the difference between right and wrong. They built the first road system ever devised for wheeled vehicles and perfected a "pony express" mail service. They had uniform coinage, standardized weights and measures, irrigation canals, and taxes.

They permitted a common language, Aramaic, not the Persian which they themselves spoke. Their objective was to accommodate the greatest number of people in the empire and so, in the long run, to accommodate themselves. At their peak the Medes and Persians demonstrated that a vast mixture of subject people and cultures, well managed and given considerable freedom, was more peaceful and more productive than a slave society. This viewpoint may seem obvious today, but it was a revolutionary idea at the time.

In a way, Cyaxares was groping toward that idea, but naturally he had no inkling of history in the making. He did not know — nor did *any* man of his time — that the world was already ancient and that in many other parts of the planet Earth groups of men were struggling with their own problems. Cyaxares would have refused to believe that there was a far-off continent, across an enormous ocean, populated by red-skinned people who had crossed over from Asia thousands of years before; that on another continent, to the south, in what we now call Peru, the highly sophisticated Chavin civilization was building elaborate temples and designing ceramics; that an advanced Nok culture flourished in what is now Nigeria; that people were worshiping strange gods at Stonehenge on an island which later would be known as England.

Cyaxares almost certainly knew little even of his nearer neighbors: emerging India, ancient China, proud Egypt. He was probably unaware that city-states were springing up in Greece. All his talents and energy were poured into the campaign against Assyria.

His triumphs of 614 B.C. gave his people new confidence. He even dressed his men to look like an army now, not just a ragtag band of herdsmen. They wore round felt caps with neck flaps; tight, long-sleeved leather tunics reaching just above the knee; laced shoes with projecting tips — the garb of men who spent most of their waking hours in the saddle. Their bows and bronze-tipped arrows were couched in elaborate cases; their spears were iron-tipped. Some wore earrings and necklaces, but it would have been worth a man's life to suggest that the Medes were sissies. In a short time they became the fiercest fighting machine in the Near East.

Babylonia was quick to recognize this, after the fall of Ashur, and to welcome an alliance with the Medes. The leaders sealed it, as was often the custom, with marriage plans. Cyaxares' baby granddaughter, Amytis, was betrothed to Nebuchadrezzar, infant son of the Babylonian king. The prospective bride and groom, even had they been old enough, would have had no say in the matter. The engagement was good for their fathers' politics, which meant it had to be good for them.

By 612 B.C. the allies were ready to mount a combined attack on Nineveh. They closed in relentlessly: The marching spearmen, the bowmen on foot, and the cavalry of archers made their deadly sweeps along the enemy flanks. Three times between June and August the armies clashed outside the city. During the third battle the Assyrians fell back inside Nineveh.

Swiftly the Medes swarmed in around the northeast Hatmati Gate, heaping the surrounding moat with stone and rubble so that they could breach the wall.  In desperation the Assyrians hastily threw up a second wall inside, but it was no use.  The Medes burst through and their revenge was terrible.  They had waited years to even the score with this longtime enemy.  A Babylonian scribe reported later, "They carried off the booty of the city, a quantity beyond reckoning, and they turned the city into ruined mounds."

Nineveh was, indeed, almost obliterated.  Palace and temples were leveled.  Thousands of clay tablets, the books of that time, were broken and scattered.  The statue of Ishtar, Assyrian goddess of victory, was plucked from its pedestal and flung headless into the dust.  Buildings were put to the torch.  Women were raped or carried off to slavery; most of the nobles were killed; artisans were pressed into forced labor to improve Media's craftsmanship.  Seldom has a people been so nearly erased from the face of the earth.

Thanks to the detective work of archaeology we can reconstruct the story of Nineveh and of other ancient citadels in this book.  Ash heaps on the site of Nineveh show us where buildings once stood and how fierce was the holocaust that destroyed them.  Scraps of brick and stone still lie in the remnants of the moat.

Archaeologists have dug through centuries of overlay to reach these and other ruins.  They have sifted out bits and pieces with a delicate touch, and by putting them together, have reconstructed the lives of vanished peoples as well as civilizations.  Between 1836 and the early 1960s archaeologists from many nations conducted more than sixty digs in the Near East.  Their findings — buildings, fragments of everyday tools and trinkets, thousands of clay tablets, scrolls, scenes, and proclamations carved in stone or metal — all of these things, plus the writings of ancient scribes and historians, when matched and critically examined by experts, have given us an intimate look at the world of the Achaemenid Empire.

So we know that Cyaxares went home with his loot on September 20, 612 B.C.  Three years later he had to march to Harran, some two hundred fifty miles northwest of Nineveh, to quash a last, stubborn Assyrian uprising. He accomplished his purpose with such ruthless efficiency that his Babylonian "allies" quaked. Captive Hebrews in Babylonia, such as the biblical prophet Isaiah, terrified their masters with predictions that they in turn would fall victims to the Medes.

"And their bows shall dash the young men to pieces," gloated Isaiah. "And they shall have no pity on the fruit of the womb; their eye shall not spare children."

The Medes didn't attack just then, but Babylon became the most heavily fortified city in the old world, to ward off not only known enemies but the "friendly" Medes.

West of Babylonia lay the Lydian Empire. For five years the Medes and Lydians waged an inconclusive war, and a senseless one if we can believe the Greek Herodotus, now dubbed the Father of History. The reason for the war, wrote Herodotus, went something like this: A number of Scythians under Cyaxares' rule used to bring game to the king from their hunting trips. One day they returned empty-handed. Cyaxares, never noted for his patience, blasted them with insults. The Scythians dreamed up a grisly revenge.

They killed a youth from the Median court, prepared and served him like game for the royal table, and were on their way to Lydia before the king discovered what he was eating. Cyaxares demanded that Lydia hand over the irreverent cutthroats. Lydia refused and the war was on.

Whether Herodotus was correct or not (Cyaxares probably needed no such excuse to go to war), the incident is plausible. Human life was cheap.

After five years of war with Lydia, Cyaxares formed another pact by marriage, wedding his son Astyages to the Lydian king's daughter. Now he could look around him with pride, for in forty years of rule Cyaxares had lifted Media from near-slavery to the role of a leading power. The Medes had taken the first long stride toward dominating their world.

chapter 2

CLUES TO THE LIFE OF A KING

ON a simmering August day in 1969 Dr. T. Cuyler Young, Jr., field director of excavations at the Godin Tepe site near Kangavar in west Iran, borrowed a donkey from one of his workmen. Legs flapping in rhythm with the beast's trot, Young rode north through a small valley and across a trickling branch of the Gamas Ab River. After several hundred yards he stopped and turned for a long-range view of the incredible structure being slowly, painstakingly uncovered by the shovels, trowels, and brushes of his archaeological crew.

Even Young — curator in charge of the West Asian Department of the Royal Ontario Museum and an archaeological "detective" in Iran for more than a decade — was awed by the sight. The Godin Tepe mound, indicating a buried habitation, had been found in 1961 during a general survey of ancient sites in the region. Four years later Young's crew had made the first exploratory dig. It was part of a larger, integrated program of field research, in cooperation with the Imperial Government of Iran and the University of Toronto, to develop in depth the human history and ecology of a single valley system in west Iran. At this point Godin Tepe seemed to be merely a watchtower.

Ancient citadels, such as Godin Tepe near Kangavar in West Iran, were often perched atop mounds to survey the countryside. Beneath this mound in 1969 archaeologist T. Cuyler Young uncovered a fortress of vast size. Royal Ontario Museum, Toronto.

After the second dig, in 1967 (Young spends alternate years back home, assessing his discoveries), Godin Tepe appeared to be a sizable manor house. Now, however, it was revealing itself as an enormous fortress from the seventh century B.C., covering an area as big as a twentieth-century football field.

Viewing it from afar on this summer day, Young was astounded. It looked exactly like ancient Assyrian reliefs of Median citadels that he'd seen. No wonder the old Assyrians had recorded such structures as this in their sculpture. Any army that could successfully storm such a fort had every right to carve a likeness of it and display it as a kind of trophy!

Luckily, as Young's crew discovered, no enemy army had ever

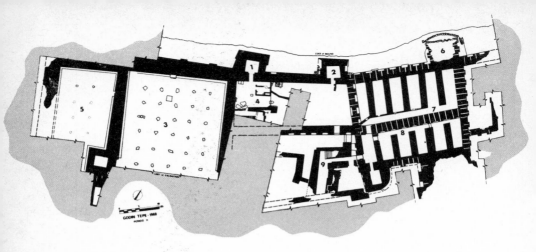

Floor plan of fortress at Godin Tepe shows audience hall where nobles held receptions and storerooms.   Royal Ontario Museum, Toronto.

ravaged Godin Tepe.  Its Median tenants, probably led by some lesser prince or chieftain, had abandoned it peacefully, perhaps moving to a bigger fort or to a city.  No matter that they took with them all the important trappings of their everyday life. Godin Tepe still tells an eloquent tale for trained eyes.  It is a unique and significant discovery, the first large-scale evidence of how the early Medes lived.

The fortress stands astride the so-called High Road leading east through the Zagros Mountains, from Baghdad to the Iranian plateau by way of Hamadan.  No caravan could pass unnoticed, no troops could sneak up unseen, for Godin Tepe was, as Young says, "like a cork in a bottle," commanding all of the valley's traffic.  Such a strategic position was essential for any leader in those times, with hostile nations or roaming bandits on every side.

Only a very powerful or very foolish enemy would have dared attack this fort.  On a mound that grew from ruins of earlier structures, dating back to about 6000 B.C., its battlements rise some twelve feet above the valley.  Seven to nine feet thick, its mud-brick walls are pitted with arrow slots, within handy reach of Median archers.  At intervals massive watchtowers jut out fifteen feet from the wall.

Snug inside fortresses like this one, the Medes lived rather well for people who, only a few generations before, had been nomads.   Godin Tepe had a kitchen with a hard floor of green limestone plaster, a pantry, and an oven room.   Steps led to a second story of private apartments built over a portion of the great storage rooms.

In the large columned hall, which was 75 feet square, the Median noble probably held receptions.   His peasant subjects must have gaped with wonder at first sight of the place.   Thirty-one wooden columns supported its ceiling, a dried mud-brick bench ran all around the room, and the noble himself sat on a raised throne at the head of the room, near a brick hearth.   Another audience hall, 40 by 75 feet, handled more intimate parties.

Obviously this Median leader could afford to live in style.   Indeed, the archaeological evidence shows that he was rich and growing steadily richer.   Inside his citadel were twelve great storerooms, some built later than others, with total space for twenty-two thousand bushels of wheat.   The storeroom doorways were too small to admit sizable articles or a tall man — Cuyler Young could barely squeeze through them.   So, very likely, they did hold some kind of grain, part of the handsome tax tribute that must have poured into this leader's treasury.

The dig at Godin Tepe reveals other facts of Median life.   The people used three grades of pottery, coarse, common, and fine,

Diagram shows how archaeologists reconstruct early pottery (right half of drawings) from shards or fragments (left half). Royal Ontario Museum, Toronto.

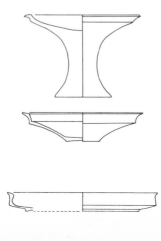
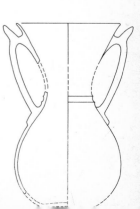

in colors ranging through brown and buff to red and gray.  Crude clay "doughnuts," believed to be weights for looms, indicate that weavers worked within those walls.  Quantities of rounded stones may have been used to grind an edge on spears, knives, and arrowheads or, more likely, were simply for slinging over the walls at enemy heads.

While part of Cuyler Young's work force of ninety-seven painstakingly bared the Median fortress, others delicately worked down into the mound for data on earlier civilizations.  In the fourth layer below the citadel they found a grim little vignette from some three thousand years ago: a skeleton sprawled in a way that suggested death had come quickly and violently.  A careful cleaning of the bones filled in the story.  A bronze arrowhead was found embedded in the ancient man's spinal column.

At the end of each season the excavators carefully distribute their artifacts.  More than half go to the Iranian government. The remainder are crated and shipped to the sponsors of the dig: The University of Toronto, the Royal Ontario Museum, the Harvie Foundation of Calgary, Alberta, and the Babylonian Collection of Yale University. The work is done in laboratories, not only on tools or fragments of pottery but on the smallest, seemingly insignificant remnants of that Median civilization, including bones and kernels of grain.  Did the Medes favor wheat, oats, or barley, and was their grain anything like ours?  Did they eat mostly goat or mutton?  Laboratory analysis of bones from the site would tell.  What kinds of wild animals roamed around them?  Already antler fragments reveal that elk, now unknown in the area, once frequented Godin Tepe.

This excavation also tells us that in such a citadel lived kings like Astyages, son of Cyaxares, although on a much grander scale.  Archaeology gives us one perspective on Astyages' life, while written history gives a glimpse of his personality, religion, and achievements.

Astyages was a weak and petulant king, with his father's violent temper but little of the old king's bravery.  Astyages' Iranian

The walls of the Godin Tepe fortress emerge under the shovels of archaeologists. Royal Ontario Museum, Toronto.

name, Arshtivaiga, meant lance-hurler, a noble-sounding name. But there was little nobility evident in his thirty-five year reign.

According to the historian Herodotus, Astyages was haunted by bad dreams. A pair of those dreams had a profound effect on history. In one nightmare, so the story goes, Astyages saw his daughter pass water in such large amounts that it swamped the whole of Asia. The king hurried to the Magi (this is the origin of our word *magic*), a caste of priests noted for their interpretation of dreams. What did the dream mean?

Early Medes and Persians always turned to their magi for spiritual advice. Their pagan world was full of friendly gods (such as Sun, Moon, Earth, Fire, Water, Wind) and evil demons, and the Magi sought the favors of the gods with bloody animal-sacrifices. With the sacrifices went a sacred intoxicating drink, *haoma*, squeezed from a plant somewhat resembling rhubarb. Often the ceremony turned into a drunken orgy.

The Medes never buried their dead. Corpses were set out to

Toy chariot in pure gold may have been a gift from Xerxes to his favorite son. British Museum.

be stripped by dogs or vultures, and only then, rid of the "polluted" dead flesh, could the bones be collected in a burial urn. The priests condoned, indeed urged, the marriage of blood relatives. They took part in the coronation of new kings, were responsible for the education of young noblemen, and were assigned as guardians of royal tombs.

The priests' interpretation of the liver of a sacrificed sheep could change a king's command. When taken out of the newly slaughtered animal, each liver was of a slightly different shape from any other, in somewhat the way that every human's fingerprints are distinctive. Over the centuries generations of Magi kept records of hundreds of such livers and of the significant events that happened after each sacrifice.

Thus, in every new liver they looked for clues from the past that would foretell the future. For example, did this liver resemble in certain ways the one taken from a sheep at a sacrifice in the year 703 B.C.? If so, did the ruler on that occasion go out afterward and win a great battle? Well then, the Magi would conclude, this was a good omen: It meant that now was a proper time for the present king to go to war.

No wonder that every word of these powerful mystics was treated with respect. When the Magi "read" a liver or translated a dream, ruler and commoner alike listened, grave and wide-eyed.

Now, said the Magi, Astyages' dream meant that someday his daughter would bear a child who would overthrow the Median empire. Astyages didn't question the prediction. His only thought was to head off this bad luck by marrying his daughter to a nobody, meaning someone other than a Mede.

Mandane, the daughter, was promptly betrothed to Cambyses, a prince of the former ruling family of Persia. Achaemenes, great-grandfather to Cambyses, had been first in the royal line; one day the entire Median-Persian empire would bear his name. At this time Cambyses was in charge of Parsumash and Parsa. He was peaceable, definitely a social inferior, and surely not likely to ever father an enemy to the Median throne. They were married and Mandane became pregnant. One night Astyages woke from another bad dream. This time he had seen a vine growing from his daughter's loins which covered all of Asia. The Magi had a ready answer: Mandane's child would usurp Astyages' throne. The king couldn't tolerate such a thought. That unborn child—his own future grandchild—had to die!

And so, relates Herodotus, when the royal baby Cyrus was born, he was secretly turned over to the king's trusted steward, Harpagus, to be murdered. Harpagus hadn't the stomach for it, so he entrusted the ugly task to a herdsman. The herdsman in turn kept and raised the boy himself, to replace his own baby, which had been stillborn.

Years later the boy Cyrus, playing the role of king in a village game, thoroughly whipped the son of a Median noble. Cyrus was hailed before Astyages to explain his insolent deed.    So manly and cool was his behavior that the king's wonder turned to suspicion—and finally he uncovered the truth.    Should Cyrus be killed? the king asked his Magi.    No, the Magi assured him. Cyrus had already been a "king," thus fulfilling their prophecy, and he was no longer a threat.    So Cyrus was restored to his parents.    As for Harpagus, who had disobeyed his monarch—his own son was slain by the king's men and served to the shocked father for dinner.

Today's historians doubt several parts of this tale.    For one thing, the story of the royal foundling is common in both fiction and fact;    Moses in the bulrushes is a biblical example.    Furthermore, Herodotus, although a diligent traveler and accurate observer of the Achaemenid Empire in the fifth century B.C., sometimes related inaccurate hearsay.

Yet even in this fanciful yarn there are clues founded in fact. Cyrus was the son of Mandane and Cambyses.    Kings of those times were strongly influenced by dreams and omens.    Human life was as disposable as chaff, and cruelty was so common that even the victims took it for granted.    Herodotus' story, if substantially true, would explain why Harpagus, who had been Astyages' close friend, later betrayed him.

Harpagus waited for years, nursing his hatred.    Finally Cyrus, in manhood, seemed to be the ideal instrument for his revenge. Harpagus persuaded several Median nobles that their tyrant king should be dethroned in favor of the Persian prince Cyrus.

Next he sent a message to Cyrus, sewn in the belly of a hare. A trusted servant, posing as a huntsman and carrying it casually slung over his shoulder like a fresh-killed game, smuggled it across the country to Cyrus.    "Son of Cambyses," the message began, "since the gods watch over you, for without them you would never have been so fortunate, punish Astyages, your would-be murderer."    Harpagus continued: "Lead the Persians to revolt, and the Median nobles will desert."

The proposition appealed to ambitious Cyrus.    To stir his

Persians to a rebellious mood he first forged an order from Astyages, appointing himself head of the Persian army.  He then
assembled men of the most influential tribes and ordered all to
appear the next day with billhooks—thick knives with curved
points.  At his command they cleared thornbushes from a vast
tract of rough land and went home exhausted.  The next day
Cyrus feted them with wine, bread, beef, and mutton.  Now, he
asked, which day did they prefer?  Naturally all votes were for
the banquet.  "Men of Persia," Cyrus cried, "listen to me.  Obey
my orders and you will be able to enjoy a thousand pleasures as
good as this!"

The troops rose enthusiastically behind him and marched on
the Medes.  Astyages sent his army to meet them—commanded
by Harpagus.  This appears to us today as incredibly bad judgment.  But the faithful retainer had served his king so long and
so well, and had taken his son's slaughter so "humbly," that Astyages apparently never dreamed Harpagus might bear a grudge.
At the field of battle Harpagus promptly led the Median nobles
over to the enemy.  Most of the remaining Medes took to their
heels.

Astyages flew into one of his famous rages and killed the Magi
who long ago had advised him to set Cyrus free.  He armed the
old men and young boys of his kingdom and personally led this
feeble force to battle.  Most of his men were killed; Astyages was
taken alive.  Harpagus was the first on hand to jeer at the prisoner.

Contrary to custom, Astyages wasn't slain.  Cyrus—great-
great-grandson of Achaemenes and soon to become the noblest
Persian of all—took the old man into the court and dealt with
him sympathetically for the remainder of his life.  It was an
unusual touch of humanity for those savage times and a sign of
better things to come.

So ended the little saga of Astyages the Mede.  His greatest
contribution to history was in losing his throne, thus opening up
a golden age both for his own people and for the Persians.

Blocks of stone, fragments of pillars are all that remain to mark the site of King Cyrus' magnificent palace at Pasargadae.

chapter 3

A TOUCH OF KINDNESS

THE proud city of Babylon was in an uproar. Barking dogs ran wildly in and out of the mud-brick houses. Chickens flew squawking from under the feet of scampering small boys. Excited men and women lined the streets. The day was October 29, 539 B.C. The new king was coming to Babylon.

At last he appeared, coming down the wide stone-and-brick "procession street" that led through the heart of the city. He rode in the middle of what seemed to be an endless column of marching infantry and prancing cavalry. Spears and armor glistened all around him. He stood straight and regal in a chariot drawn by eight splendid white horses. From time to time he lifted his arm in solemn greeting. His lean, imperious face, with its thin lips and finely sculptured nose, looked out on the people, unsmiling but benevolent. The cheers became deafening. Hundreds of admirers strewed green branches in his path — the ancient version of the "red carpet."

But this was Cyrus, the Persian conqueror! Why were the Babylonians greeting him with cheers instead of spears and arrows? Because not only had he promised to treat them with kindness, he also had persuaded them that he was no alien con-

Two guards, a Persian (right) and a Median (left), are shown in bas relief from palace stairway at Persepolis. Note differences in dress. Oriental Institute, University of Chicago.

queror, but rather the rightful king of Babylon. Such was the success story of Cyrus, a born diplomat and manager, and perhaps the first great propagandist in history.

Like Cyaxares before him, Cyrus used his head as well as his sword. He tempered his thirty-year rule (559–529 B.C.) with wisdom and tact. He believed in retaining the best features of the culture from every conquered land and in allowing the captive peoples a degree of freedom. This was the philosophy that made the Achaemenid Empire great, and Cyrus was its first practitioner on a large scale.

This lion was an enamelled decoration on the walls of Babylon. The lion, the bull and the snake were three animals sacred to Marduk, protector of Babylon. British Museum.

He put his philosophy to work from the moment he defeated his Median grandfather, Astyages, and permitted him to live. And although Media was beaten, its capital, Ecbatana, became a favorite royal residence.

In peace the Medes were on an equal footing with the Persians. They were frequently appointed to high office in civic government and posts of leadership in the Persian army. Foreigners referred to the Medes and Persians, making no distinction between conquered and conqueror. Indeed, where only one term was used to describe them, it was usually "the Medes."

By taking Media, Cyrus automatically inherited Median claims to a part of Assyria and that portion of Asia Minor as far as the Halys River, all strung out to the northwest of Persia toward the Black Sea. Babylonia, however, immediately to the west, as well as Egypt and Lydia, in western Asia Minor, were all vying with Media for power. If Cyrus expected to extend his empire, he would have to fight three rivals. United, they could have beaten him. But part of Cyrus' genius was the ability to divide and conquer.

He studied Babylonia and decided to bypass it for the moment. It was too formidable. Instead, he turned away from the poplars,

cypresses, and plane trees of the uplands and marched down into the hot Mesopotamian plain.

He won his way easily through Assyria, for it was already a Median dependency. Nevertheless, travel was so slow and communications so poor that a ruler never knew what was happening on the outskirts of his realm. It was always wise to march out periodically and slap down rebellious subjects.

By 548 B.C. Cyrus was ready to press on against Lydia. And what a prize it was! Croesus, king of Lydia, ruled most of Asia Minor from the Aegean coast on the west to the Halys River in what is now Turkey. He was so incredibly rich with plunder, mostly from Greece, that even today the simile "as rich as Croesus" is part of our language. Appropriately, his only lasting contribution to history was a two-part coinage system: Coins of pure gold and pure silver (at a fixed proportion of three to forty) replaced the single coin of white gold.

Croesus' offering to the oracle, or soothsayer, on the eve of the Persian war is a clue to the size of his well-stuffed treasury. He sent the oracle one hundred seventeen gold ingots, each 18 inches long, 9 inches wide, and 3 inches thick, and weighing from 114 to 142 pounds. He added two huge mixing bowls, one of pure

Stylistic rendering of popular animals—lion, deer and ibexes —as shown on this bronze vase (circa 1,000 B.C.) was typical of the Achaemenid artistry. British Museum.

gold weighing a quarter-ton, one of silver with a 5,000-gallon capacity. For good measure he threw in a gold statue of a lion weighing 750 pounds, a pure gold figure of a woman 4½ feet high, and various minor trinkets.

In return for all of this the Lydian king did receive an accurate forecast. If Croesus fought the Persians, predicted the oracle, he would destroy a great empire. The oracle failed to make clear whose empire would be ruined.

Meanwhile, shrewd Cyrus saw a chance to avoid bloodshed with a little gentle persuasion. He had cut off the route of possible aid to Lydia from Egypt or Babylon and he was therefore in a strong bargaining position. Cyrus made an offer. If Croesus would bow to Persian sovereignty, he would be permitted to stay on his Lydian throne. Croesus, misunderstanding his oracle's forecast and confident of victory, refused.

On a May morning in 547 the two armies came face to face. There was a sharp battle. Both sides lost a number of men and both withdrew that night. When Cyrus did not resume the fight in the morning, Croesus pulled back, assuming the enemy had had enough. The Lydian marched home and disbanded his forces. He planned a leisurely winter. He would call on the Spartans, Egyptians, and Babylonians for aid. Then, in the following spring, they would all march together to destroy this bothersome Persian.

But Cyrus was not the sort to wait while an adversary marshaled his strength. To the Lydians' astonishment, he followed them. So swiftly did he swoop down upon them that one morning he was at the outskirts of Sardis without warning. Shocked though they were, the Lydians were no cowards. They rallied their excellent cavalrymen, famed for their extra-long spears. It was clear to Cyrus that a grim fight lay ahead of him.

Then his faithful Median retainer, Harpagus — who had once served another king — spoke up.

"Put your men on camels, sire!" he said. Camels, he explained, looked so strange, smelled so bad, and made such peculiar noises that horses invariably bolted at sight of them. It was an outlandish suggestion, but Cyrus never turned away from a bright idea. He brought up all the humpbacked beasts from his baggage train and hoisted soldiers onto their backs (an experience that must have unnerved more than one simple Persian cavalryman). Off they plodded toward the enemy, with surprising speed. Sure enough, the Lydian horses stampeded. Their riders dismounted and fought gallantly on foot, but they were pushed back into the city.

The siege of Sardis was on. Under no conditions, Cyrus warned his troops, was Croesus to be killed if captured. On the fourteenth day, Cyrus, like any good twentieth-century businessman, introduced the incentive system. His officers rode through the ranks with a message from the king: "The first man to climb the walls gets a reward from Cyrus."

Some of the troops immediately tried a mass assault and were beaten off. Then a soldier named Hyroeades, idly gazing at the steepest side of the stronghold — a combination of wall and precipitous cliff that both armies assumed was impossible to climb — saw a strange sight. A Lydian defender lost his helmet over the side, clambered part way down to recover it, and managed to scramble up again. The wall could be climbed and Lydian defenses would be thin on that side!  Hyroeades led a party of men up cliff and wall and caught the Lydians totally by surprise. He managed to open a gate and let the rest of Cyrus' army in. The Persians swarmed through Sardis.

One soldier attacked the Lydian king, so Herodotus relates, and not recognizing him, raised his sword to strike.  Suddenly Croesus' son, who had been mute since birth, cried out, "That is Croesus!  Do not kill him!"  Miraculously, he had gained the power of speech and saved his father's life in one instant of terror.

Then, according to one account, Croesus committed suicide on a funeral pyre to avoid the indignities and torture he expected to receive.  This practice was customary among captured kings. But Herodotus insists that Cyrus spared Croesus and kept him at court.  This version, too, is plausible, for it would be characteristic of the tolerance Cyrus showed his fallen enemies.

When Lydia collapsed, the Ionian and coastal Greek cities fell too.  They accepted Persian rule, paid tribute, and from that time on furnished regular quotas of soldiers.  Even so, Cyrus left them a vestige of self-government.  Each city was ruled by a Greek, although he was always selected by the Persians.

Still with an eye on Babylonia, Cyrus marched east.  He added a string of new provinces to his collection and built fortified towns to protect them from fierce Asiatic tribes.  He had by now almost doubled the area of his empire, but not its wealth.  He felt strong enough to take prosperous Babylonia even if it chose to resist.

In earlier times Babylonia would have fought to the death. Nebuchadrezzar had made that empire feared and hated, most of all by the captive Hebrews.  When the Hebrews rebelled, he carried off their princes, craftsmen, and soldiers.  When they rebelled again, he burned Jerusalem.  The Hebrew king Jehoiachin and his sons were used as an example to the Hebrews.  The king's sons were slain before his eyes and he was blinded.  He and thousands of his people were then hauled into Babylon.  It was Nebuchadrezzar who forced the Jews to worship golden images.  It was he who cast Shadrach, Meshach, and Abednego

This impressive gateway in the southern walls of Babylon, protected by Ishtar, goddess of love and war, has been well preserved. British Museum.

into a fiery furnace, only to see them come out unscathed. (This story is told by the biblical prophet Daniel.)

Babylon! What a prize it must have seemed to Cyrus! In Nebuchadrezzar's day the very name had signified pomp and power. Jeremiah the prophet, although he hated the place, grudgingly called it, "a golden cup in the Lord's hand, that made all the earth drunken." Years later Herodotus admiringly said, "It surpasses in splendor any city of the known world."

Here was the famous Tower of Babel, which was actually a ziggurat, or terraced pyramidal temple. In Babylon, too, were the Hanging Gardens—acre upon acre of terraced park, built by Nebuchadrezzar to remind his homesick Median queen, Amytis (Cyrus' aunt), of the hills of home.

As for the city itself, a series of archaeological digs conducted between 1899 and 1918 have left us a vivid picture. Babylon was a major town by ancient standards. It covered about five hundred acres, had a normal population of probably one hundred thousand, and was bisected by the Euphrates River. The city proper was surrounded by an inner wall. Then came a kind of suburban area, mostly houses of mud or huts of reed scattered among palm trees. Surrounding this was an outer wall about ten miles around.

The walls of Babylon were legendary even in their time. They were of sun-dried and oven-burnt brick, heavily reinforced with towers and an escarpment (steep embankment of earth). The outer wall was thirty-six feet wide, roomy enough to accommodate two four-horse chariots abreast. Thus troops could be moved swiftly to any point in the defense system.

A visitor's eye immediately fell upon the great Ishtar Gate of burnt brick, more than 36 feet high, decorated with 575 brick-relief dragons and bulls. Through this gate ran the half-mile procession street, 63 feet wide, paved with red and white slabs of stone, and with 120 brick lions posed along its flanked walls. Down this street marched kings and armies, past the bowing populace and into the 13-acre palace grounds. Here 5 blocks of buildings clustered around a vast central courtyard. The throne room alone was 180 feet square and finished in blue glazed brick. The palace had its own stout defenses: a canal, enormous bastions, and a huge buttressed wall.

In physical structure Babylon seemed to be impregnable. But its heart and courage were gone. Nebuchadrezzar was dead now. Misrule and graft were everywhere. The miserable peasants were neglecting their fields to such an extent that by 546 B.C. Babylonia actually faced a famine. The king, Nabonidus, was preoccupied with archaeology and the search for ancient monuments. The fiery Jewish prophets, still seething in their captivity, were already proclaiming Cyrus as the Lord's anointed and their deliverer. "Jehovah saith of Cyrus, He is my shepherd and shall perform all my pleasure," wrote Isaiah.

Thus, when Cyrus set out with his armies in the autumn of 539, he was marching toward a sick nation. Along the way he put to the torch the city of Opis, in that part of northern Babylonia called Akkad, wiping out the town and its people. The psychological effect of this terrible deed was the last straw for the Babylonians. The city fell almost without a struggle. Only the royal citadel held out for a few days.

Now, in the hour of his triumph, Cyrus showed his genius as diplomat and propagandist. He treated the captured king, Nabonidus, with dignity. When Nabonidus died the next year, Cyrus led the state in official mourning. In the temples worship went on as usual. No Persian soldier was permitted to bear arms within their sacred walls. Indeed, Cyrus sent back to the temples many statues of gods that Nabonidus had brought into the capital. Under Gobryas, the Persian administrator in charge of Babylonia, most of the former officials retained their posts. And at the great annual New Year festival Cyrus clasped the hand of the statue of the god Marduk (or Bel, the westernized name), thus legalizing his rule.

Proclamations were issued by every king in those times, as an official laying down of the law. But there was a subtle difference in the one Cyrus issued in Babylon. It was really a propaganda piece, preserved for us on a clay tablet, recounting the sins and errors of the old king and telling how the gods, looking around for a "righteous prince," chose noble Cyrus.

I am Cyrus, king of the universe, great king, mighty king, king of Babylon. [That was a clever touch. He always claimed to be king of Babylon, not just some Persian interloper.] . . . king of the world quarters, seed of sovereignty from old, whose rule Bel and Nabu love, over whose sovereignty they rejoice in their hearts. [If both of those gods rejoiced, no Babylonian was going to argue with them!]

My numerous troops marched peacefully into Babylon. In all Sumer and Akkad I permitted no unfriendly treatment . . . [Cyrus seemed to have forgotten about those fires in Akkad.] The dishonoring yoke was removed from them. Their fallen dwellings I restored; I cleared out the ruins. . . .

So it went on and on, this written statement for the educated classes in their own language. For the common folk a simpler version was prepared in Babylonian verse, to be shouted and sung across the land. People swallowed it at home and abroad. The psychological victory far exceeded in scope the military conquest. Babylonia was still a symbol of power in the ancient world and Cyrus had won it. Lesser monarchs, led by the king of Syria, hastened to pay their respects.

Cyrus, to his credit, didn't abuse his new powers. He adopted Aramaic as the official language of the Persians in their dealings with the western provinces, although he could have insisted on Persian. He established himself for all time as a benefactor of the Jews. Back in Ecbatana in 538, he decreed:

As for the house of God which is at Jerusalem, let the house be built, the place where they offer fire sacrifice continually; its height shall be ninety feet and its breadth ninety feet with three courses of great stones and one of timber. And let its cost be given from the king's house. Also let the gold and silver utensils of the house of God, which Nebuchadrezzar took from the house of God and brought to Babylon, be restored and brought again to the temple which is in Jerusalem, each to its place. And you shall put them in the house of God.

So the captive Jews were free to go home. In 537 B.C. more than forty thousand of them joyously trekked back to Jerusalem, their promised land, to rebuild the temple. A high Persian officer went along to see that the royal orders were carried out. Cyrus was not altogether unselfish in this act. Palestine was on the route to Egypt; when someday he set out to conquer the pharaoh, it would be nice to have friends along the way.

Cyrus was now head of the greatest empire ever known to man. To rule a land so vast required new governing techniques. He replaced nations and states with twenty satrapies, each ruled by a satrap ("protector of the kingdom"). A satrap, in practice, was a minor king. Sometimes this situation went to his head and he developed delusions of grandeur. To keep him under the royal thumb, his secretary, chief financial officer, and the general in charge of the local garrison all reported directly to Cyrus. In addition, Cyrus' personal watchdog, called the king's eye or king's ear, made a yearly inspection of each province.

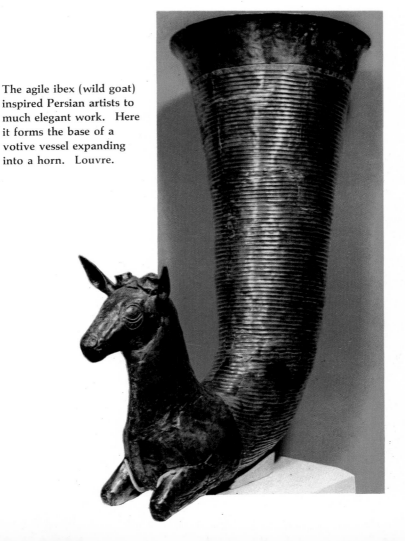

The agile ibex (wild goat) inspired Persian artists to much elegant work. Here it forms the base of a votive vessel expanding into a horn. Louvre.

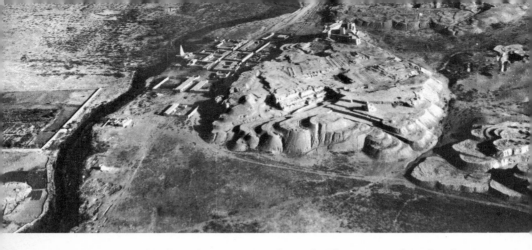

The original palace of Cyrus was at Susa, the Elamite capital on the plain of what is now Khuzistan. Oriental Institute, University of Chicago.

Cyrus at last had some free time for building palaces, a favorite pastime of the Achaemenids. He already had the royal quarters at Ecbatana, of course, plus his own original palace at Susa, not to mention the handsome quarters in Babylon. But his architectural contribution to history was his residence at Pasargadae.

It was to be a kind of retreat, in the heart of his homeland. He chose a site in a mountain-enclosed valley southeast of Ecbatana, sixty-three hundred feet above sea level. Its built-up area extended one and a half miles. Outside the palace complex were undoubtedly the tents and wooden dwellings.

The palace area, inside mud-brick walls on stone foundations about thirteen feet high, had three major buildings. There was an enormous gatehouse, a palace called the audience hall, and a second palace, which was probably residential. They were well separated by patches of shade trees, gardens, and flower beds watered by little brooks. There were dozens of majestic columns, topped with carved bulls and lions. Portions of walls, finished in a kind of stucco, were vividly painted in lapis lazuli blue, turquoise green, copper red, crimson, and yellow.

Here the king, in gold-embroidered robes, received visitors, relaxed, or worshiped at the fire altar. Here, too, like every man yearning to be remembered forever, Cyrus prepared his tomb. In 529 the Massagetae, a fierce but relatively minor tribe of nomads, were located east of the lands of Cyrus. They lived and dressed somewhat like the bandit Scythians, and were led by a savage queen, Tomyris. When they began staging forays against his northeastern frontier, Cyrus decided to punish them personally. Leaving Cambyses at home, the aging king crossed the Araxes River (Araks River in the southern U.S.S.R.).

Here Herodotus takes up the tale, a strange one indeed. Cyrus marched for a day into Massagetae territory, laid out a sumptuous banquet, then withdrew most of his force, leaving a feeble detachment behind. About one third of Tomyris' troops fell into his trap—for trap it was. They killed the little band of Persians, sat down to the food and wine, ate and drank too much, and fell asleep.

The Persian army returned, slaughtered many of the Massagetae, and captured others, including the queen's son. The young man begged to be freed from his chains. Cyrus granted his wish, and the prince promptly committed suicide.

Now the nomad queen attacked in real fury. The armies clashed head on, first in a rain of arrows, then hand to hand with spear and dagger. The battle was long, brutal, and inconclusive. But when it was over, Cyrus was dead.

Then, writes Herodotus, Tomyris sent for Cyrus' body, severed the head, dropped it into a skin bag brimming with blood, and cried, "Now have your fill of blood!" So died the king of kings, victim of a relatively minor battle.

Cambyses came to take the body home to the tomb in Pa-

Cyrus prepared his own burial place while he was still alive, a massive block of granite with four huge steps leading up to it. Oriental Institute, University of Chicago.

sargadae.   The man known to the Persians as "father" and to the Jews as "anointed of the Lord" was carried through a stone door into a windowless chamber 10½ by 7½ feet in area and 8 feet high.   There, by flickering torches, his body was placed in a gold sarcophagus on a funeral couch with legs of gold.

On a neighboring table were the offerings: short Persian swords, necklaces, gems set in gold, tapestries, trousers, blue and purple robes, so that Cyrus might enter the afterworld properly equipped.   Close by, the attendants built a small guardhouse for the Magi who would constantly watch over his grave and each month sacrifice a horse to their dead leader.

On the tomb itself was the simple inscription "Here I lie, Cyrus, king of kings."   It was enough.   All his people knew and would remember him.   He was the king who built an empire, and who introduced to his little world a new trait in the art of ruling: generosity.

These massive edifices are the tombs of several Persian kings, such as Artaxerxes, Cyrus I, Darius I and Darius II.   The tombs are near the palace at Pasargadae.   Oriental Institute, University of Chicago.

chapter 4

HOW THE EMPIRE WORKED
AND PLAYED

THE Babylonian thief Gimillu was a thorough and unrepentant rascal. In the years of graft and mismanagement before Cyrus' conquest of Babylon, Gimillu stole copiously, whatever, wherever, and whenever he pleased.

One day he boldly helped himself to sheep from the pastures of the temple of Eanna. (Temples were major landholders and livestock owners in those times.) On another occasion he ordered his own shepherd to steal five mother ewes from a different temple. Once he sent his brother to seize a temple goat from a flock at the very gates of their Babylonian city, Uruk.

Although crime was his main occupation, Gimillu officially was a serf in the employ of one of the temples. Once, the temple governor ordered his serf to take prisoner a shepherd who was tardy in submitting his annual tribute of sheep to the gods. Naturally, Gimillu made the most of his assignment.

First he extorted from the shepherd, in return for a promise of protection, one sheep, ten *kur* of barley (about forty bushels), and two silver shekels (which would buy four bushels of barley and six bushels of dates—two months' food for a large family).

Then Gimillu put the shepherd's son in iron fetters as punishment for cheating the temple.

At last, with the reign of Cyrus, justice caught up with the thief. In September, 538 B.C., Gimillu went to trial before the assembly, council, and high officials of Uruk. It took four scribes to keep up with the testimony, as witness after witness described Gimillu's black deeds. Even the thief himself admitted blithely one charge: "That young lamb I took. But I left two sheep for holy day!" Again, to demonstrate what a decent fellow he really was, Gimillu told how he stole a sheep but passed up a chance to take two silver shekels and a goat!

The court ruled that Gimillu must make restitution: 60 animals for every one he stole. The fine totaled 92 cows, 302 sheep, and one pound and 10 shekels of silver. Gimillu appealed to the satrapal court in Babylon. He lost again, and was detained in Babylon to make amends. But soon, by flattering and bribing his superiors, Gimillu was home again and presumably up to his old tricks.

His story is intriguing in several ways. It shows us that the Achaemenids had all the human failings common to any other

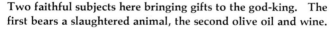

Two faithful subjects here bringing gifts to the god-king. The first bears a slaughtered animal, the second olive oil and wine.

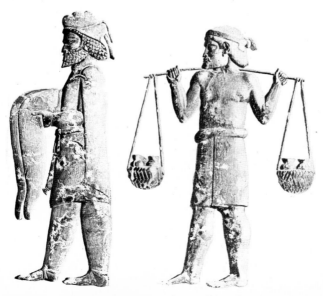

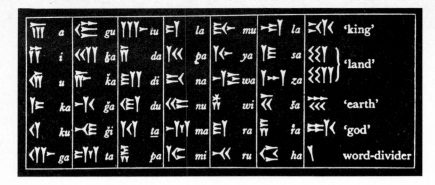

(Above) Example of primitive Persian writing from the fifth century B.C. (Right) Example of Persian writing of the Achaemenid period in cuneiform characters. British Museum.

age. It offers a glimpse of Cyrus' judicial system. But the most remarkable fact is that Gimillu's tale even exists, and exists in such detail. It comes to us through letters and commercial documents, all on clay tablets recovered from various archaeological digs. More than a half million such tablets have been recovered within the last century, from sites that once were part of the Achaemenid Empire. Nearly all are in two of the prevailing languages of that period, Elamite (Elam was a Persian province) and Akkadian.

In Cyrus' time the Achaemenids spoke Old Persian and sometimes used it in cuneiform on royal inscriptions. The script consisted of straight lines and angles impressed on clay by a sharp-edged stylus or chiseled in stone. They also kept some records in Elamite on clay. Akkadian, a dying language from ancient Mesopotamia, was still used for record-keeping in many parts of the empire, also in cuneiform on clay.

The Hebrews spoke Hebrew. But Aramaic, a Semitic language with a flowing script that resembled modern Hebrew, was spreading through the empire. It was widely understood and Cyrus and his successors let it become the everyday language. Many business records were in Aramaic on parchment.

Generally, only professional scribes could read and write. Even kings weren't always literate. Much of the scribes' instruction in their art was verbal, which also helped to develop their memories. A scribe needed an agile mind. In cuneiform writing, a sign could be read as either a word or a syllable, each with different phonetic values. The scribes had to master more than one language. But thanks to their diligence and the Babylonian fondness for records, we have a history of their time.

Twenty-five centuries before Cyrus the Babylonians understood bookkeeping and were marking their business transactions in cuneiform. As a result of these records we can now estimate the value of money in the Achaemenid Empire. The silver shekel was the most common coin. An ordinary laborer earned about one and one-half shekels a month. We know that this was a bare subsistence wage.

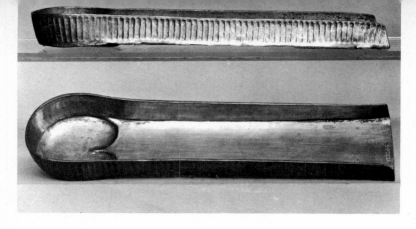

These two views of a silver scoop show how Achaemenid artisans imbued even everyday objects with beauty. British Museum.

A similar workman in the Middle East today earns approximately $21. So, very approximately, the shekel was worth $13 in terms of modern buying power. The talent, of which we'll hear much more and which equaled 3,600 shekels, could therefore be estimated at about $47,000 in modern terms.

We turn to the Babylonian records for other intimate pictures of everyday life among the Achaemenids. The clay tablets not only extend our knowledge but enable us to confirm or correct the writings of such ancient historians as Herodotus. With all these records to guide us, we shall now take a trip through the heart of the empire.

We are on the fiercely hot plain that lies between the Tigris and Euphrates rivers, north of the Persian Gulf. Nature is not particularly kind to this part of the world. A mere fifteen inches of rain fall here in a year. The wind seems to blow eternally from the northwest in summer and southeast in winter. But at first glance Babylonia appears busy and prosperous. Green rows of palms, heavy with dates, line the banks of the Tigris, Euphrates, and the twinkling blue irrigation canals. Irrigated fields are golden with barley, sometimes as much as twelve thousand gur (roughly fifty thousand bushels) to a single large estate. This is primarily agricultural land; farming is still regarded as man's basic and most worthy occupation.

Small industry and crafts have flourished for a long time,

though, in towns and on large estates.   Artisans are making
tunics, trousers, shoes, jewelry, furniture, and vessels of gold,
silver, and bronze.   Sailing ships and camel trains bring copper,
iron, and silver from Cyprus; honey, dyes, and alum from Egypt;
cedar and teak from Lebanon.   Workmen are busy on roads and
canals.   The Achaemenid Empire seems to have nourished industry in Babylonia.

Babylonia, in turn, has given its new masters much knowledge.
Long before the Persians arrived, Babylonians understood math-
ematics and used reference tables for multiplication and division,
squares and cubes, square and cube roots.   In geometry they had
discovered the theorem for the right-angled triangle.   Mathe-
matical problems were being solved with methods much like
those used in modern algebra.

"I have added 7 times the side of my square and 11 times
its surface," goes a problem on one of the clay tablets of the
time.   "The result is 6,15 [in sexagesimal numeration].   Write
down 7 and 11."   In effect, the Babylonians had set up the
equation:  $11x^2 \times 7x = 6, 15$.

Babylonian astronomers studied the stars with the naked eye
and gave constellations names that endured ever after: the

(Left) Bronze bowl with ibex from the Achaemenid
period.  Levy Collection, Geneva.  (Right) Persian
pitcher is made of gold.  British Museum.

Twins, the Scorpion, the Lion, the Fish, the Goat, and others. They divided the year into months, although not as precisely as the Egyptians. The Babylonian year was three hundred sixty days. Periodically they had to insert an extra month to make their year match the course of the sun and seasons.

Babylonians knew and practiced medicine, too, as did the Assyrians. Drugs were administered as potions, inhalations, enemas, suppositories, liniments, poultices, and ointments. Some of them are still recognizable. For instance, a remedy for urinary retention went: "Crush poppy seeds in beer and make the patient drink it. Grind some myrrh, mix it with oil, and blow it into his urethra with a tube of bronze. Give the patient some anemone crushed in *alappanu*-beer."

Mercury, antimony, arsenic, and sulphur were incorporated in medicines. Wounds were cauterized with heat and sometimes taped or stitched. The physician had absorbent lint, linen swabs, and bandages; knew something of the brain and spinal cord; and was aware of the pumping heart and the pulse.

But now, as we tour the empire, we notice that all of this knowledge is for the trained and privileged few. As for that outpouring of goods and farm produce, little finds its way to the average Babylonian, either as food or money. It is becoming clear that Babylonians, with reportedly the highest standard of living in the empire (except for tax-free Persia itself), fall within two main groups, with all the benefits going to the rich.

Looking more critically, we find a pecking order—clearly defined social levels. On top, naturally, are the royalty and the court. Courtiers aren't necessarily of noble birth or of long-established "society" families. Being a close friend of the current king is credential enough.

Babylonian nobles may be part of the court through their one-time status in the old Chaldean society, or they may simply fit into the next social rank of aristocrats who hold most of the important offices. These upper classes meet in formal assembly to make judicial decisions under the watchful eye of the "king's

A rectangular metal plaque from the seventh century, B.C. showing
an aurora surrounding the head of a man holding a lamb.  British
Museum.

headman," a sort of prosecuting attorney. Everyday administration is left to the council, made up of twenty-five leading men of the community.

Nobles are full-fledged citizens and property owners, which makes them very important persons. Only rich individuals and the wealthy, all-powerful temples can afford choice cultivated land. Between the reigns of Cyrus and Darius the price of land quadrupled to as much as three shekels per *qa* (675 square feet). Undesirable and uncultivated land goes for as little as eleven qa for one shekel.

Other, less noble, Babylonian citizens — bankers, merchants, priests, and temple or government officials — form an upper middle class, likewise highly privileged. Brewers, butchers, carpenters, bakers, artisans, and the like are labeled as citizens, too, but are socially a notch lower. These tradesmen, however, are a step up the status ladder from another classification, the unskilled free laborer, although their rates of pay are about the same. A free laborer, hiring out to help build a canal or reap a barley crop, can expect a shekel and a half a month.

Actually the laborer rarely lays eyes on his shekel. His monthly wage is entered in his employer's books. Taking goods against his balance, he is generally overdrawn and forever in debt. In reality he is no better off than the next man down the status line, the serf. Serfs receive no pay but some are lucky enough to rent small farms by giving a share of the produce to the owner. Thus they are assured of food and a shelter. Some freemen dedicate their children to serfdom; it can be a better life than their own.

**Silver spoon from the fifth century B.C. is typical of Achaemenid artistry. British Museum.**

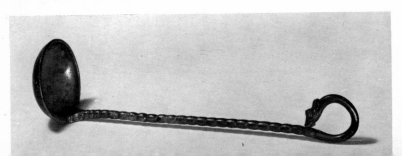

Most of these people live in homes of sun-dried mud-brick. Some occupy a bare one-room hut with mud floor, blank walls, and a sort of vestibule built around the open doorway to shield the interior from prying eyes.

A middle-class family may have several small rooms, all facing a tiny inner courtyard. They spend most of their day in this paved courtyard, taking to the dreary small rooms only to escape rain or the fiercest midday sun, or to sleep on a bed of cushions. They cook in open kettles in brick ovens or on the surface of large pottery jars, laid on their sides, with small fires burning inside.

Imported lumber is far too expensive for ordinary homes. Only temples, palaces, and mansions of the very rich include cypress (one shekel per beam), cedar (one shekel per ten pounds), or stone quarried, hauled, and cut at enormous cost. Middle-class families can sometimes afford oven-baked brick (fifty to a hundred for one shekel) laid together with sticky bitumen (tar) freighted down the Euphrates River by boat, at about one shekel per six hundred pounds.

But the matter of building one's house is really academic; few can ever own a home. The average price of house and lot has tripled under the Achaemenids, to forty shekels a reed (ten and one-half feet). So nearly everyone rents (at least in the city) at rates as high as twenty shekels a year, payable in advance in two installments, at the beginning of the first and seventh months. Nobody dreams of asking the landlord to make repairs. The tenant patches his own roof and walls.

Everywhere there is a double standard of living. Along the city streets stroll elegant, perfumed men, sometimes carrying ornately carved walking-sticks, greeting their fellows with a kiss on the cheek. They wear linen tunics and slippers; in cooler weather they will add a woolen cloak, perhaps gaily colored. They glitter with earrings and bracelets. Their women wear eye shadow, glass beads, and rings from Egypt.

But the average man? No linen for him! The cultivation of

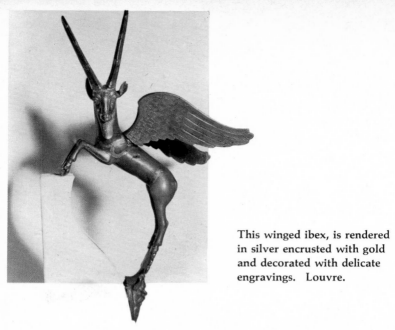

This winged ibex, is rendered in silver encrusted with gold and decorated with delicate engravings. Louvre.

flax, common in Egypt, is just beginning in small gardens in Babylonia; a hundred stalks costs one shekel. So commoners wear a plain, drab cloak of wool or goat hair, a garment to accommodate all seasons. Even wool is expensive but it is necessary because the only household fuel is dried animal dung or the fast-burning thornbush, scant comfort in the short but cold winter. Two pounds of wool costs a month's wages. A pound dyed in purple costs fifteen shekels. Only the rich or royalty can afford the precious purple because the dye comes from a rare Mediterranean shellfish, and each shellfish provides only a drop.

The temples also own or buy most of the cattle, donkeys, mules, and horses — partly for business transactions, partly to have a steady supply of sacrifices. Animals for sacrifices must be perfect and for these the temples pay wildly inflated prices. We learn of a horse sold for nearly four pounds of silver, the amount of a laborer's wages for twenty years. A donkey might sell for ten shekels or even a hundred.

We understand now why the working classes rarely have meat on their tables; they're lucky to find a goose or a duck for special occasions. A prominent Persian, however, can eat mutton or goat fairly regularly and can celebrate his birthday by roasting a whole ox, horse, camel, or donkey, following it up with assorted desserts. His guests toast him in fine imported wines, floated downriver from Armenia in casks aboard little round boats made of animal hides stretched over wooden frames.

But a good grape wine costs eight shekels. Laborers therefore content themselves with cheap beer or a jug of home brew from the upper shoots of the date palm. It's too sweet and gives them headaches, but it costs slightly less than a month's wages.

From their plain clay utensils the working families eat mostly dates and flat unleavened barley bread. The grinding stone to make flour is a standard household item. Those who live near the gulf or a river may have an occasional fresh or dried fish. No wonder so many people reek of garlic. It's cheap and it enlivens the dreary diet. A clay tablet tells of a wholesale purchase of 395,000 bunches of garlic, to be sold over the counter in small shops. Most people also like sesame seed oil (a substitute for fat), but a bushel of seed costs two month's pay.

All in all, it is a tedious, grinding kind of life. Wages and prices are more or less standardized, true, eliminating some of the former abuses. But wages are low, and staying low, while prices and taxes are steadily rising.

Taxes, the curse of the common man! Taxes to subsidize the high-living royal court; taxes to build roads that are mostly used by the nobility or the rich; taxes to clothe and feed armies (but what use is the splendor of armies when one is barely eking out a living?). Taxes on estates, fields, gardens, flocks, mines, flax, dates. A tax for transport along the canals. A fee for entering the gates of Babylon. And for those who can't pay taxes, there is forced labor for upkeep of canals.

So most people are caught in a whirlwind of inflation. But the bankers and loan businesses are flourishing. The temples lend money, too, as well as barley, dates, and other goods to their peasants, who must pay up at harvest times. The peasants are forever in the temple's clutches, living from debt to debt, year after year.

The interest rate for a loan from a temple or private bank is 20 percent. Sometimes a creditor will accept a "pledge" in lieu of interest. It might be the use of one of the debtor's household slaves or a house or a plot of land during the course of the loan, which he will return if the debtor pays up in time. Sometimes both interest and pledge are demanded. Sometimes interest must be paid by the month, which vastly multiplies the 20-percent rate.

Many people are swamped in debt. Some are only now making the final payments on farms purchased by their grandfathers. Yet they are struggling along from birth to marriage to death; what else is there to do? Disease or improper diet prevents most people from reaching old age — which is just as well for them. In Bactria, claims Herodotus, the old and sick are thrown to a "burial detail" of savage dogs while still alive. In another region people over seventy are left in the desert to starve. In still another, seventy-year-old men are killed and eaten by their relatives, and old women are strangled and buried.

At least in his lifetime every man can aspire to some sort of marriage. A slave will be mated with the bride of his master's choice. A freeman can attend the annual sales held by some villages, at which all girls of marriageable age are auctioned off. Wealthy men pay good prices for pretty girls. This money, in turn, goes to poor men who are paid to take away ugly or crippled women.

Death, birth, marriage, all the natural events of life, are welcomed. They are the poor man's entertainment. A wedding or funeral provides an excuse for a social gathering and a modest feast. The arrival of a visitor is likewise the signal for laying out the best available food and drink. Simple conversation is perhaps the greatest pleasure of all. It costs nothing and it lingers in the courtyard for hours on end.

Such was everyday life in the empire. It was much like life anywhere, anytime: good for the rich, bad for the poor, and unfortunate for the homely woman.

chapter 5

# HOW HISTORY CLEARED
# CAMBYSES' NAME

O N March 27, 538 B.C.
—New Year's Day in the ancient empire—the citizens of Babylon
again lined the streets in holiday mood to cheer royalty. This
time they were saluting crown prince Cambyses, who was per-
forming the first New Year's Day rites since the conquest.

New Year's was by far the most important festival of the
year, and Babylonia was the most important satrapy. So the
mere fact that Cambyses was there, standing in for his father,
Cyrus, who was home in Ecbatana, signified that here was the
favorite son and future monarch.

Down the famous procession street rode the prince, to the
temple of the god Nabu. There he bestowed gifts of food and
money on the priests, clasped the hand of the statue of Nabu,
and in return was awarded the "scepter of righteousness."
Then, with Nabu carried reverently beside him, Cambyses
moved solemnly to the statue of the great god Marduk. He
presented the scepter to Marduk and bowed low. The priests
handed the scepter back on the god's behalf. Through Cambyses, the gods officially endorsed Cyrus' title as king of Babylon.

The story of Cambyses is an instructive example of how a man
can acquire in his own time a reputation he doesn't deserve,

Smiling statuette is of the god
Nabu from about the ninth
century, B.C. Although he
is the protector of both
scribes and priests, there is
nothing solemn about him.
Only his crown suggests his
divine traits. Louvre.

and how archaeology and history can later shine the light of
truth on people as well as places. Of all of the Achaemenid leaders Cambyses was the most unfairly judged by gossips in his
own time and by historians immediately after his death.

Cambyses got the reputation of being stupid and irresponsible, even mad. But now that we know a little of the truth, from Egyptian papyri and from the precious clay tablets that reveal so much about events in the empire, a new Cambyses emerges. Just as the sifting of evidence can clear innocent people in modern mystery stories, so a patient study of facts from long ago shows that Cambyses, a better than average king, was the victim of bad luck and bad publicity.

In fact, he was neither mad nor particularly inept. But an Achaemenid king, like any leader at any time in history, was forever in the spotlight. When things went well, he was a hero. When his luck turned bad, he was a villain.

Usually history tells little of an Asian crown prince of this period. For the most part he was tucked away in the harem with his brothers and half brothers until it was time to take the throne. Then he often had to fight for the crown against various pretenders.

Not so with Cambyses. To avoid intrigues, Cyrus wisely named his oldest son as crown prince at the time he took over Babylon. His proclamation to the Babylonians cited Cambyses as king's son and stated that Marduk had blessed Cyrus and Cambyses "while we before him with sincerity, joyously praised his exalted godhead."

Then Cyrus went home, leaving Cambyses, already a mature man, as his personal representative. The clay tablets tell us that the prince worked diligently at his role for eight years. He quietly set up his headquarters, not in Babylon, but in the city of Sippar, farther north. Wisely he retained on his personal staff many palace dignitaries from the old Babylonian regime. Documents refer to Cambyses' steward and to one of his slaves who was an expert stonemason, able to instruct others in the trade.

When Cyrus marched off to his fatal battle with the Massagetae, he appointed Cambyses as his regent, with formal permission to use the title "king of Babylon." Upon Cyrus' death Cambyses automatically inherited the empire.

It must have been difficult for a son to grow up in the shadow of Cyrus, so wise, so capable, and so beloved by the people. But in Babylon, at least, the new king was already well liked.

Elsewhere, the death of Cyrus made some subject nations restive. They tested the new leader, to see if he would measure up. If he didn't, they would soon break away.

The Greeks, for example, were sharply critical when Cambyses, on taking the throne, married his sisters Atossa and Roxana. This was Persian custom and even the Magi condoned it. But the Greeks didn't believe in incestuous marriage.

Evidently there were other rumblings in the kingdom, because four years passed before Cambyses could resume the plan to conquer Egypt. Presumably he had to consolidate his father's gains and put down other contenders to the throne. One persistent story, recorded by his successor Darius, maintains that Cambyses had his brother Smerdis assassinated because the latter coveted the throne. Murdering one's brother—or any family member if expedient—was common enough at the time. It is quite possible that Cambyses did this and kept it a secret from all but a few close associates in the palace.

One way or another, Cambyses tidied his affairs by 526 B.C. and was off to Egypt. We know little of his journey except that it surely must have been an ordeal for troops who had never before crossed the Sinai Desert. Cambyses had exchanged a pact of friendship with the Arab leaders, however. The latter stationed camel trains, with skin bags full of water, at strategic points along the way. Probably this more than anything else enabled the Persians to survive.

We know even less of Cambyses' actual campaign, except that the Egyptians were no match for his well-drilled Persian troops. He won three successive battles and by May of 525 had made himself ruler of Egypt.

Cambyses then marched on up the Nile. Suddenly the campaign began to go wrong. His supplies ran out and he failed to sweep southern Ethiopia, which had been next on his schedule.

Map shows the extent of the Achaemenid Empire at its peak. Oriental Institute, University of Chicago.

It was even rumored that his starving troops resorted to cannibalism. On a separate expedition a sandstorm swooped down and swallowed up one of his armies, which was trying to take the remote Oasis of Ammon.

Such misfortune, caused by his own bad management, undoubtedly sharpened his temper. But now, according to stories collected by Herodotus, Cambyses was painted as a vicious madman. It was said that he violated the corpse of an earlier Egyptian king; that he stabbed and killed Apis, the sacred bull of Egypt; that he mocked religious customs; treated priests with violence; desecrated images and temples; and interfered with religious festivals. One tale depicted him wantonly shooting an arrow through a boy's heart in an argument with the boy's father. Another claimed he murdered one of his wives, who had accompanied him to Egypt. It was said he even tried to shoot down the faithful old retainer Croesus, who was still playing lapdog to the Persian court, but that Croesus took to his heels and got out of range.

There must have been a little truth in the welter of tales. Any ruler in those times had to be harsh to survive. And since Cambyses lacked the style and skill of his father, he undoubtedly overcompensated with violence.

But some of the criticism has been shown to be slander. Certain Egyptian priests were told, in effect, to fend for themselves. Cambyses gave them marshland sites where they could cut their own timber for firewood and boats. He reduced their cattle award by half. On the matter of fowl, he ordered, "Give them not to them. Let the priests raise geese and give them to their gods." None of this was calculated to make him popular with the priests, but the order sounds like a straightforward economy measure.

In the major Egyptian temple at the delta city of Saïs, seat of the dynasty he had just overthrown, Cambyses was a model of decorum. He worshiped and made offerings to the goddess Neith and other Egyptian deities. Feasts and processions were revived in their original form. Cambyses himself offered sacrifices like any Egyptian king. As for the sacred bull that he allegedly stabbed, historians searching ancient records have learned that the beast in question died while Cambyses was on his ill-fated trip into Ethiopia.

A limestone relief of the period shows Cambyses in native royal costume, worshiping the deceased bull. At the king's bidding, Egyptian craftsmen made textiles, amulets, and ornaments dear to Egyptian hearts, all for the bull's funeral.

Cambyses also sent out for building materials to restore temples. He adopted the Egyptian name Mesuti-re, "son of Re, Cambyses, dedicated, who is given all life, all stability and good fortune, all health, all gladness, appearing as king of Upper and Lower Egypt, forever." When Egyptians complained that Greek mercenaries had settled in their temples, Cambyses ordered them thrown out, destroyed their houses and goods, and restored all temples to their former state. It was a proper thing to do, but naturally it gave him a bad name among the Greeks.

It would appear, then, that Cambyses' religious conduct was

impeccable, that he was acting precisely as his father would have done.   He applied the same creative management and the same tolerance toward subject people, and he left them their institutions.   There was no hint of revolt among the Egyptians when Cambyses headed toward home in 522 B.C.

But more troubles awaited him.   Alas, he had stayed away too long.   In his absence a pretender to his throne had arisen.   The man posed as Cambyses' brother Smerdis and was said to resemble him.   The pretender was probably a Magus who knew of the murder of the true Smerdis and had decided to capitalize on it.

One story has it that Cambyses, upon hearing of the pretender, became depressed and committed suicide.   Herodotus maintains that the king, when he heard of the threat to his throne, sprang angrily to his saddle.   In the scramble he lost the cap to his sword sheath, accidentally pierced his thigh, and subsequently died of the wound.

The intrigues of his reign did not end with his death.   The pretender held the throne for several months.   Then a band of seven conspirators, all of them Persian nobles convinced that their ruler was not the royal Smerdis and fearing a ruling clique of Magi, talked their way past the palace guards.   They fought through a handful of protective eunuchs and stabbed the Magus and his brother in a bloody struggle.   According to Herodotus, they then rushed into the streets waving the severed heads of the Magi, shouted the story to the people, and set off a brief purge, with bloodthirsty Persians slaughtering any Magi they found.   One of the plotters, Darius, moved up to the throne.

Cambyses' name faded from sight.   He was never a hero in the memories of his people, but neither was he as bad as he was painted.   He not only kept the empire together, but also added vast, rich Egypt to it.   Had he not been chronologically caught between two such giants as Cyrus and Darius, Cambyses might have left his name on more palaces and in more memories.   As it is, history has at least set his record straight.

chapter 6

PROPHET FROM THE HILLS

This I ask thee, tell me truly, Ahura:
How should prayer be made to one like you?
As to a friend, Mazda, teach thou me.

T HIS is the plea of a
prophet to his god. The prophet is Zoroaster, the god is Ahura
Mazda (literally, "Wise Lord"), and the cry comes down from
the sixth century B.C. In his lifetime Zoroaster was a significant
and controversial figure. Even today we find traces of his influence in modern Buddhism and Christianity.

Indeed there is more than one similarity between Jesus Christ
and that prophet of the Medes and Persians. Zoroaster, too, was
hated by many in his time, for he preached against the entire
religious establishment. He spurned devil worship and he believed in one god, whose prime interest was man's good behavior.

To appreciate how revolutionary this was, we must understand
the prevailing religion of that time. The early Iranians practiced
a crude polytheism, meaning they worshiped a host of gods and
lesser demons. Many of the gods were nature deities. There
was Mah (the moon), whose changing phases helped govern
planting times; Vayu (the wind), whose gentleness or bitterness
governed a Persian's fortune; Atar (the fire), who helped sacrifices find their way to the gods. One of the most important
pre-Zoroastrian deities was Mithra, whose fame and significance
actually survived the efforts of the prophet to be rid of him.

Ahura Mazda, the Zoroastrian god of light, was portrayed this way in the palace of Darius, sixth or fifth century, B.C.   Louvre.

Mithra was closely associated with the sun, was a protector of pastures and homes, and played an important role in seeing that people kept their oaths as given in business contracts or political treaties.  If Mithra liked a man, he would bless him with cattle, male children, beautiful women, and chariots.  Mithra was all-seeing and all-knowing.  Any poor peasant who had been cheated or robbed could pray to Mithra.  If his plea was righteous, the god would smite the offender with powerful punishment — leprosy, for instance.

The early Medes and Persians believed that they could please and control these gods through bloody animal sacrifices.  Wearing a crown of myrtle, the sacrificer — generally one of the Magi — led the beast to the ritual place, called out the name of the god, slaughtered and cut up the creature, and boiled the flesh.  The pieces were then piled on a layer of tender herbs, usually alfalfa, and the Magus chanted a hymn or incantation.  Afterward the sacrificer could do as he pleased with the flesh.  Sometimes during the ceremony the participants drank haoma, and the ritual turned into a noisy party.

Zoroaster deplored these savage sacrifices and he called haoma a "filthy intoxicating drink." Thus it is easy to imagine the scorn and threats the Magi must have heaped on him. But the enlightened Persian kings allowed the teachings of Zoroaster to spread in the empire — just as they permitted other ideas and customs to flourish — and reaped the benefits.

The principles of Zoroastrianism helped make the empire a better place in which to live. Eventually the Achaemenids themselves officially adopted a form of Zoroastrianism as their royal religion, thus putting the seal of approval on Zoroaster's teachings and contributing greatly to the survival of his prophecy.

Zoroaster has been called a magician, astrologer, quack, witch doctor, politician — even a myth. We know little enough of him as a person. The best guess is that he was born into a simple country family in northwestern Media around the end of the seventh century B.C., preached his religious message in northeastern Iran, and lived to be about seventy-seven years of age. We learn nothing of his looks and little of his youth, except that he was born Zarathustra (which meant "with golden camels"), son of Pourushaspa ("with gray horses") and Dughdhova ("who has milked white cows"). "Zoroaster" is a westernized version of his Iranian name.

In the early years of his preaching, the prophet lived in fear of persecution. His fears were later set down in the Avesta (a sacred collection of his thoughts and of Zoroastrian hymns, legends, and theological treatises):

> To what land to flee, whither to flee shall I go?
> From nobles and priestly colleagues they separate me.
> Nor are the peasants to me pleasing,
> Nor yet the Liar princes of the land.
> How am I to please thee, Ahura Mazda?

Zoroaster fled to the northeast, to approximately the area where modern Iran, Afghanistan, and the Soviet Union meet. Here he succeeded in converting the wife of the local ruler to his new teaching and eventually converted the ruler, Vishtaspa,

hymns and songs probably written by Zoroaster himself.    A second part, *Yashts* and ancillary texts are a series of hymns directed to various deities.    The third part, *Videvdat*, means "Law against the Demons."    With the exception of the "Gathas," the Avesta represents a stage of Zoroastrianism later than that preached by the prophet and shows how his teachings were revised through time.

Because later Zoroastrianism was so much changed from what the prophet taught, and because the texts mainly date from this later time, it is difficult to know exactly what Zoroaster himself did teach and believe in.    Certainly he respected fire, the representation of truth, and the fire altar became a symbol of his cult.    (Zoroastrians later were incorrectly called fire worshipers, though in fact this was merely a byproduct of their religion.)

Pastoral life had a strong influence on Zoroaster's thought. He classed neglectful farmers, along with tyrant kings and dishonest judges, as evil men.    Perhaps because of his rural upbringing, he believed men owed kindness to animals.    Agriculture was a noble occupation; dumb animals did the hard work and so should be revered.

In this gold plaque the king is trying to kill the lion with his dagger.  The scene is also symbolic of the eternal struggle between good and evil, a dominant theme in Persian religion.  Louvre.

Probably Zoroaster did preach against animal sacrifice and the drunken haoma cult, but soon after his death a compromise with the old ways had to be effected. Animal sacrifice and haoma, practiced in a much more restrained way, became a part of orthodox Zoroastrianism. Later Zoroastrians always stunned the sacrificial beast before killing it with a knife.

Certainly the Zoroastrianism that the Achaemenid kings knew was a religion already much changed from the original belief of the prophet. Darius, the powerful king who succeeded Cambyses, was probably a Zoroastrian. At least he worshiped Ahura Mazda, apparently exclusively, spoke out strongly against the Lie, and denounced the Unjust in a tone very like Zoroaster's.

Outside of Iran, Darius praised Ahura Mazda but paid lip service to "the other gods that are." But Darius, canny in the Achaemenid tradition, may have done so chiefly to keep all his captive peoples happy.

The religion went on changing through the centuries, just as any religion does. In time it became the state religion of later Iranian kingdoms, particularly of the Sassanian dynasty, reigning several hundred years after the death of Christ. But today it is officially represented by only a remnant of believers.

Nevertheless, the spirit of Zoroaster's teachings reached far. Elements of his gentleness and his protests against unrighteousness showed up in Buddhism, which originally arose in India about the fifth century B.C., and has since become the faith of millions. His principles contributed greatly to the climate of religious thought that influenced postbiblical Judaism and the rise of Christianity. The three wise men who followed the star to the baby Jesus in Bethlehem were probably Magi of the Zoroastrian faith. And there are reflections of Zoroastrianism in the Christian belief in one God, the distinction between right and wrong, and the faith in a life after death.

All of us today may owe more than we shall ever know to the gentle prophet from the Median hills.

chapter 7

# THE ROYAL MANAGEMENT MAN

HIGH on a cliff at Behistun in western Iran, sixty-five miles southwest of Hamadan, a strange monument looks down on the world, as it has since five centuries before Christ. Carved into the sheer face of a mountain, it is the official biography and portrait of an Achaemenid king—Darius, successor to Cambyses.

The memorial stands more than two hundred feet above the old caravan route from Babylon. To be sure that no vandal or graffiti artist could climb up to deface it, Darius had the rock cut smooth immediately under it. The British archaeologists who found it in 1836 knew they had discovered a treasure. Not only was it a rare record of a great Persian ruler, but it would prove to be an "open sesame" to other discoveries. The Behistun inscription is trilingual—repeated in Old Persian, Elamite, and Akkadian. It thus gives historians an invaluable key to those languages, enabling them to match known words, syllables, and characters in one against their counterparts in another.

The autobiography originally went out in more portable form —probably in cuneiform tablets, Aramaic scrolls, and by word of mouth—in the autumn of 520 B.C. It reached every part of the empire. A carved inscription dug up from Babylonian ruins is in Akkadian.  A papyrus from Egypt is in Aramaic.  But the message in all of them is the same.  "Saith Darius the King . . ." begin most of the paragraphs of self-praise and reportage.

Every man of the realm, if he knew what was good for him, learned those pearls of wisdom by heart.  When Darius the King spoke, the subjects snapped to attention.  In just two years since he became king he had whipped a restless empire into a smooth-running, obedient machine.  Already he had served notice that he would be the greatest king of all.

Darius' subjects probably never knew that he did not personally compose his autobiography.  But the sentence "It was inscribed and read off before me" convinces latter-day scholars that some nameless scribe, after a careful briefing from the king, pulled together the glowing account.  Darius would have had a

This enamelled representation of a griffon, a mythological animal, was one of many used to embellish the walls of Darius' palace at Susa.  Greek influence is clearly visible.  Louvre.

The inscriptions on the famous Behistun Rock fascinated British archaeologist Henry Rawlinson who had workmen climb the face of the rock to get copies of them. Courtesy, George C. Cameron, University of Michigan and the American Schools of Oriental Research.

ghost-writer in his organization, just as any contemporary manager would in our own time. The king had a flair for law, a talent for finance, an innate sense of leadership. Transplanted into the twentieth century, he would immediately have dominated Wall Street or soared to the top of some international corporation. As it was, he brought the Achaemenid Empire to an all-time high.

Like most ghost-written pieces, the autobiography was dressed up and, in some details, was inaccurate. Difficulties were glossed over. Victories were made to seem easier than they were in actual fact. But it became one of the most important records of the time, partly because the Behistun 10-by-18-foot stone-relief portrait is our first truly detailed look at a Persian king.

He was a handsome Aryan, five foot ten, with a high forehead and a straight nose. His hair, fashionably frizzed in front and gathered in a bunch at the back, was topped with a gold band studded with jewels and rosettes. His drooping moustache twirled at the tips and his square beard hung in four rows of curls, as was the Persian royal custom. A robe with wrist-length

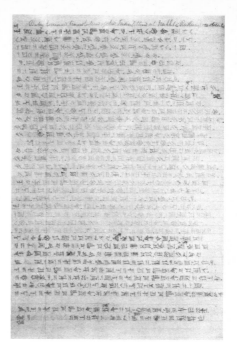

Page from Rawlinson's journal contains Babylonian translation of ancient hieroglyphs, only one line in English. British Museum.

sleeves covered most of his body, showing a glimpse of trousers and low-laced shoes.

How did this virtual unknown at age twenty-eight seize the greatest throne in the world? Through a mixture of quick wits, nerve, and the element of ruthlessness that every conqueror finds essential. Though not a direct successor to Cambyses, he was a distant cousin, one of a parallel line descended from Achaemenes. He was born Darayavaush ("who sustains good thought"), son of Hystaspes. Darius joined Cambyses' Egyptian expedition and worked his way up to become head of the royal bodyguard.

Young Darius was the most active and vocal of the seven conspirators, according to Herodotus. He actually struck down the Magus who snatched Cambyses' throne. Afterward, claims the "Father of History," the seven were more or less in accord on how the kingdom should be run. They had a measure of mutual respect and agreed to choose a king from among themselves by omen. At dawn they would mount their horses at the

Homely, everyday objects like this silver handle were beautifully made. British Museum.

city outskirts; he whose horse neighed first after sunrise would automatically become king.

Darius was not one to leave things to chance. He told the plan to his groom, who being a Darius-man, was an idea-man. That night the groom tethered a mare at the morning meeting-place and let Darius' stallion mount her. At sunup the candidates for king rode to the spot. Darius' horse, immediately recognizing the scene, neighed excitedly. The other riders sprang from their saddles and bowed to the ground before Darius the King.

This particular Herodotus story is almost too much to swallow. If the throne was won that easily, however, Darius more than earned it in the next two years. He took over an empire flaring in rebellion. Satraps and pretender kings were openly defiant. Darius fought nineteen battles and defeated nine "kings." These were battles for survival and the loser was invariably slain after some exquisite torture. Fravartish, a Median rebel, for example, had his nose, ears, and tongue cut off and his eyes put out. He was displayed to his followers in this state.

The fanatical loyalty of Darius' followers helped the young king, too. His friend Zopyrus was a case in point. Rebellious Babylon had braced itself for a long siege, even going to the lengths of killing off most of its women to save food. For once Darius seemed to be thwarted. Then Zopyrus made a supreme sacrifice. He deliberately cut off his nose and ears, shaved his head like a criminal's, raised welts on his body with a whip, and "fled" to Babylon, posing as a man mutilated by Darius and seeking revenge.

The Babylonians didn't entirely trust him, but they decided to put him to the test. They sent him out at the head of a small force to engage the Persians. Zopyrus won, just as he and Darius had planned, for Darius deliberately sent a thousand of his own men to certain death, armed only with daggers. A second and third time the Babylonians tested Zopyrus. Each time, Darius allowed him to slaughter more Persian troops.

But now the trap was set. Zopyrus, the sudden hero of Babylon, was made general in chief and guardian of the wall. Now it was easy for him to let Darius' legions in. The conquering king decided that Babylon needed a lesson. He smashed and burned the defenses to the ground, pulled down the gates, and impaled

Stylized birds (top of vase) and geometric designs rendered in striking black against ivory background were characteristic of Persian pottery. This vase, found at Susa, dates back to the fourth century B.C. British Museum.

three thousand leading citizens. Then he made Zopyrus governor for life and even exempted him forever from paying taxes.

Now the entire empire knew who was boss. Darius was able to settle down and turn his mind to administration. He knew he could not go on holding power by sheer force. But neither was he willing to adopt the too-liberal policies of Cyrus or the absentee-management program of Cambyses. Darius was convinced that only his Persians could be trusted. They must be the masters. Local people would retain much freedom, however, in the tolerant Achaemenid tradition. (Since they outnumbered the Persians, this also was sensible.) They would keep their own language, institutions, and religion and share in whatever benefits their province produced. But the twenty satrapies, unlike those of Cyrus, would always have a Persian satrap, someone from the nobility or even the royal family itself.

This system required supervision. The satrap had absolute civil authority and considerable military power. Persian or not, he might grow independent and greedy. Darius was quite aware of this and set up controls to prevent it. Next to each satrap

A weight stone recovered from Persepolis, is believed to have been used by Darius. It was valuable to archaeologists because of its inscriptions in Elamite, old Persian, and Babylonian. Oriental Institute, University of Chicago.

was the local army commander in chief, directly responsible to the king. The local tax-collector was also the king's man, making sure that all forms of tribute made no detours before reaching the royal treasury. A secretary at the satrap's elbow was liaison to the king. At any time the king's eye might glower down on all of them. This eye — a high official or perhaps a brother or son of Darius — toured the empire continuously, with his own army if necessary, dropping in for unannounced checkups and putting the fear of the Wise Lord into the satraps.

Darius, to his credit, didn't depend on terror alone. He made laws. Formal law wasn't new to the world; Darius probably borrowed liberally from older legal codes, such as that of a famous Babylonian king, Hammurabi, who lived about 1700 B.C. That code was actually a collection of key decisions put down on stone and kept in temple libraries through the centuries as a guide to other lawmakers. Today we possess Hammurabi's casebook almost intact because the original stone carving, or stele, on which it was written was unearthed by French excavators at Susa in Iran.

Hammurabi's law stressed that "the strong should not injure the weak" and that they should "give justice to the orphan and the widow. . . . Let any oppressed man who has a case come before the image of me, the king of righteousness."

Darius was evidently much influenced by the Hammurabi casebook. Although archaeologists have yet to find a copy of Darius' laws, called the *Ordinance of Good Regulations,* they have found references to it in various Babylonian and Akkadian tablets and on some royal inscriptions.

From these we learn the Achaemenid king's personal credo: "What is right I love and what is not right I hate. The man who decides for the Lie I hate. . . . And whoever injures, according to what he has injured I punish. . . . Of the man who speaks against the truth, never do I trust a word." Darius deemed it particularly important that "the stronger does not smite nor destroy the weak."

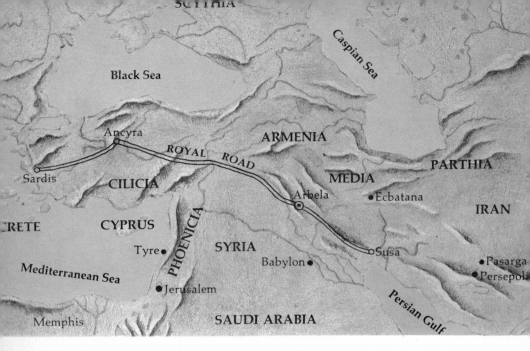

Darius' royal road ran for a distance of 1,677 miles from Sardis on the Mediterranean to the palace at Susa. Only through fast communication assured by a good road system was Darius able to maintain personal control over his far-flung satrapies.

The first example in Hammurabi's casebook dealt with the importance of evidence. Similarly, Darius ruled, "What a man says against a man does not convince me until he satisfies the *Ordinance of Good Regulations*." In other words, hearsay was not enough to convict an accused person. So even without a copy of the *Ordinance* we know the general tone of justice during Darius' reign.

The laws were relayed throughout the empire in Aramaic, on baked tablets, leather scrolls, parchment, and stone. They were thoroughly feared and respected. The biblical Book of Daniel refers to "the law of the Medes and Persians, which alters not" and notes that "no edict or statute which the king establishes may be changed." Punishment was harsh. An offense against king or state could mean death. Lesser criminals might get off with mutilated hands, feet, or eyes. The king's appointed judges had to pay strict attention to evidence and be incorruptible.

Cambyses had set a pattern here.   One of his judges took a bribe to give an unjust ruling.   Cambyses had him slaughtered like a sheep, flayed, and his skin tanned in strips to cover the judgment seat — a warning to his son, who was the next occupant of that seat.   Likewise, Darius sentenced a dishonest judge to crucifixion, literally taking him down from the cross only after considering another of the king's laws — that one wrong deed in a man's life might be pardoned if it was outweighed by a record of good.

The hand of Darius even fell on our thieving old acquaintance Gimillu.   In November of 521 B.C., so a series of Babylonian clay documents tells us, Gimillu was cheating and stealing as busily as ever.   Although still a serf in the employ of the temple in Uruk, he apparently had been given a great deal of responsibility. He had received a thousand kur of seed barley, two hundred oxen to work the irrigation machines (probably some form of water-wheel or bucket lift), and the iron for making those machines. In return, the serf was to furnish the Uruk temple with ten thousand kur of barley and twelve thousand kur of dates.

Harvest time came; Gimillu went back on his bargain.   He demanded six hundred oxen, another thousand kur of barley, and four hundred peasants.   This was outright extortion and in earlier years it might have worked.   But now the Persian administrators simply found another serf with a more reasonable bid. Gimillu not only lost his job but had to flee for fear of arrest — and vanished forever from Babylonian records.

Enforcing the law through scattered local officials would have been impossible had the king not maintained personal control. This, in turn, called for constant communications between the palace and the satrapies, and good communications in Achaemenid times could be provided by only one thing: good roads.

Lesser empires had fallen apart for lack of a fast-moving message or army.   Darius, the management man, made his Royal Road a model of its time.   It ran 1,677 miles from Susa, the capital near the Persian Gulf, to Sardis in one-time Lydia, almost within sight of Greece.  Fresh horses and men waited at all times at 111 post stations along the way.  The wheel-ruts were paved in stone and the whole route was marked off in *parasangs,* a measurement of usually a little over three miles.  Strictly speaking, a parasang was the measure of an hour's traveling time, which varied in different parts of the trail.

Along this marvelous road, kept free of bandits and well stocked with inns for food and rest, sped the king's messengers.  Day and night they rode, and from Herodotus' description of their dependable service comes a phrase often adapted to postmen in a later day: "These are stayed neither by snow nor rain nor heat nor darkness from accomplishing their appointed course with all speed."

The messages themselves were sometimes inscribed on tablets and signed by rolling a cylinder seal upon the clay.  The seal bore the royal crest or initials or some other distinctive symbol of the signer.  Sometimes the documents were in Aramaic written in ink on papyrus, parchment, or hide.  These were rolled up, the scroll was tied with a ribbon sealed with clay, and the signature seal was imprinted on the clay.

In a week the king's word could be sped across his empire.  Private correspondence and private travelers were free to use the road.  They were carefully scrutinized by the king's officers, however.  Here was yet another way in which Darius kept his finger on the national pulse.

Caravans made the trip from Susa to Sardis in about three months, excellent mileage in those times.  So the road helped

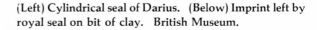
(Left) Cylindrical seal of Darius.  (Below) Imprint left by royal seal on bit of clay.  British Museum.

the flow of commerce. A remarkable flow it was too, stimulated by Darius' tireless interest in everything. Agriculture intrigued him and he deliberately set about cross-fertilizing the many regional specialties that abounded in the empire, thus giving all subjects a better-balanced standard of living. Lucerne, excellent horse fodder from the Median valley, found its way to Greece. Domestic fowl, white doves, and peacocks from Asia were introduced to Europe. Pistachios were planted at Aleppo; sesame seed was imported to Egypt; eastern trees and fruit were transplanted in the west; rice was taken into Mesopotamia.

Darius the agriculturist; Darius the communicator; Darius the lawmaker—was there anything the man couldn't do? He saw to the building of irrigation systems in the Syrian desert, harbors on the Persian Gulf, and a canal from the Nile to Suez. He standardized weights and measures. The king's measure— about a bushel in our terms—supplanted various private measures. The royal cubit was set at precisely eighteen inches; the *karsha,* about a fifth of our pound, was taken as a standard in weight. He regulated coinage. The daric was set at 98 percent pure gold, the shekel had to be at least 90 percent refined silver, and the ratio of silver to gold in value was set at 13.3 to 1.

Like every king, Darius was especially fond of taxation. His taxes were usually fair, based on exact measurement of the subject lands and their relative fertility. (An unfair exception was Persia proper, which paid no tax.) The yearly income amounted to about 14,560 talents. All of this poured into Susa to support the royal court (nearly a thousand people) and the armies. Any

**Coins like these were found by archaeologists in the palace complex at Persepolis. Darius standardized coinage, expediting trade. Oriental Institute, University of Chicago.**

This is one figure out of a procession of archers adorning the walls of the palace at Susa. The archers are the famous Immortals of the Imperial Guard. British Museum.

surplus went into the king's reserve fund. There were also payments in kind: horses, cattle, and food that helped support the satraps and their hangers-on. For instance, the tiny satrapy of Cappadocia on the southeast shore of the Black Sea each year contributed 1,500 horses, 50,000 sheep, and 2,000 mules.

One good illustration of how the subject nations handed over manpower and goods without question, and how this paid off for the king, is set forth in Darius' own account of how Susa's palace was built. It is also a lesson in building construction, as practiced by the ancients. The story is lovingly told in Old Persian cuneiform on a clay tablet dug out of a foundation box at Susa. Other texts of the same document, in all three official languages, were found elsewhere in the ruins.

> From afar its ornamentation was brought . . . Downward the earth was dug until I reached rock in the earth. When the excavation had been made, then rubble was packed down, one part 40 cubits in depth, another 20 cubits in depth. On that rubble the palace was constructed.
>
> And that the earth was dug downward, and that the rubble was packed down, and that the sun-dried brick was molded, the Babylonian people it did [the work]. The cedar timber, this —a mountain by name Lebanon—from there was brought; the Assyrian people brought it to Babylon; from Babylon the Carians and the Ionians brought it to Susa.
>
> The yaka [teakwood] was brought from Gandara and from Carmania. The gold was brought from Sardis and from Bactria, which here was wrought. The precious stone lapis lazuli and carnelian which was wrought here, this was brought from Sogdiana. The precious stone turquoise, this was brought from Chorasmia, which was wrought here. The silver and the copper were brought from Egypt.
>
> The ornamentation with which the wall was adorned, that from Ionia was brought. The ivory which was wrought here was brought from Ethiopia and from Sind [India] and from Arachosia. The stone columns which were here wrought, a village in Elam from there were brought.
>
> The stonecutters who wrought the stone, these were Ionians

This bronze cup dates back to the thirteenth century, B.C. It is one of many artifacts found at Luristan, the "doorway to Asia," all done with great skill, probably by nomads. British Museum.

and Sardians. The goldsmiths who wrought the gold, those were Medes and Egyptians. The men who wrought the baked brick, those were Babylonians. The men who adorned the wall, those were Medes and Egyptians. Saith Darius the King: At Susa a very excellent work was ordered; very excellent it was. Me may Ahura Mazda protect, and Hystaspes my father, and my country.

The account is also a geography lesson on the Achaemenid realm. Sardis and Caria were in what is now Turkey. Ionia was on the east coast of the Aegean. Carmania was in what is now southern Iran. Chorasmia and Bactria were around the Aral Sea, now part of the Soviet Union, and Gandara was immediately to their south. Arachosia lay in what is now eastern Iran and western Afghanistan.

Thus did the people of the empire bend their backs and empty their coffers for the king. What did they get in return? An element of peace, a degree of individuality, and orderly management. But even in Darius' time, prices took such a drastic jump that the good life was losing its former charm.

It was probably as good a life as the people had known under any previous regime, and far better than what lay ahead. But it was best of all for satraps, nobles, and the king. Darius, as we shall see, managed to surround himself with an ultimate piece of elegance that made Pasargadae and even Susa look like low-cost housing.

chapter **8**

A PLACE IN THE COUNTRY

B<small>Y</small> early November 1932, Ernst Herzfeld, the bald, mild-looking professor of Oriental Archaeology from the University of Berlin, sensed that he was on the verge of an enormous discovery. His archaeological crew was at work in a dry, sunbaked Iranian valley northeast of Shiraz, about one hundred fifty miles due east of the Persian Gulf. They were in the second year of a dig sponsored by Chicago's Oriental Institute. Slowly, with infinite care and patience, they were laying bare Persepolis, the colossal spring palace of the Achaemenid kings.

For centuries travelers had gazed in wonder at the visible remains of the palace—a few upright stone-columns, much fallen statuary, and a great mound of firmly packed rubble at the foot of the Mountain of Mercy. In 1621 a Roman nobleman had accurately identified it as an ancient Persian capital. In the nineteenth century two or three parties had made tentative digs. Generations of nomads, terrified at the sight of huge, grotesque winged animals carved from stone, had given the ruins a wide berth. Herzfeld himself, with thirty years' experience in Iran, had thoroughly surveyed the site. Now he was literally getting to the bottom of it.

The magnificent stone palace at Persepolis was begun by Darius I and finished during the reign of his grandson, Artaxerxes. With the palace completed, the political and artistic life of Persia began its shift to what is now the Iranian plain. Reliefs show Assyrian influence. British Museum.

In the first season, 1931, the crew had cleared and renovated much of the royal harem — tiers of stone and mud-brick apartments that the expedition began using as living quarters. Early in 1932 they had found the outline of a palace proper (one of several, it seemed), discovered stairs leading into a council hall, excavated more of the harem, and removed debris from the audience hall that had occupied a platform some ten feet higher than the vast terrace on which the entire complex stood. But where were the stairs that, logically, should be attached to the platform? None were visible.

Herzfeld doggedly began the search. "There *must* be stairways leading up here!" Down, down they went, through rubble twenty-six feet deep in places. In November the crew made an incredible find.

There were stairs on two sides of the platform, with those on the east side perfectly preserved by layers of crumbled mud-brick and rubble. But most exciting were the magnificent carvings in stone all along the face and side of each stairway — a stone-relief story of a New Year's Day festival at Persepolis, a complete picture of Darius' court and visiting representatives from his subject lands.

All told, there were a thousand linear feet of carving and sculpture, averaging six feet in height, beautifully preserved from the elements by layers of rubble. In a few days Herzfeld had virtually doubled the world's existing discoveries of this particular Achaemenid art!

There was more to come. Excavations continued. (They went on until 1939.) During that time Herzfeld and his successor Erich Schmidt found more than thirty thousand clay tablets in cuneiform — by far the biggest single discovery of its kind in

Aerial view of a palace uncovered by an archaeological dig. Oriental Institute, University of Chicago.

Iran. They cleared the royal treasury, more of the terrace, and part of the *apadana,* or audience hall. While digging for stairs, they found another marvel: a vast, complicated underground drainage-system.

Every ounce of earth was sifted for beads, gold, bronze, pottery, jewelry, and tools. Many such bits of everyday living were found. Every kind of material and soil was studied by experts and some was chemically analyzed.

The Iranian government subsequently continued excavation and analysis of the site. Today Persepolis stands partly restored, an awesome skeleton at the foot of the mountain, its stone "bones" tinged with gold or silver by the light of sun or moon. The stairways and the vast terrace are all cleared. The harem has been rebuilt and the outlines of all other major buildings are delineated. The framework of gates and doorways stands tall and lonely, while skilled masons, with chisels driven by compressed air, carve replicas of missing architectural pieces. Damaged reliefs, columns, and capitals have been patched with cement of a matching color. A few of the towering columns soar to their full height, like trees stripped bare by a forest fire. In every main building the bases of columns stick up like small stumps, indicating how the building once looked. Now we know how and why Persepolis was built, how it was used, and how it looked to the kings who occupied it.

Persepolis at its peak was an incredible forest of buildings. There was the apadana, a throne hall, harem, treasury, three separate palaces, a garrison for the guard, the complex of stairs, and a couple of huge gates. Darius probably began planning it in 520 B.C., as soon as he had sorted out his newly acquired empire. The work went on for sixty years, into the reign of his grandson Artaxerxes—and no wonder, for the task would have

(Overleaf) Summer palace of Persepolis as it looks today, partially restored, a forest of towering columns and pediments of columns. In its rubble, sculptures, bas reliefs, statues, fragments of walls and clay tables, have all been found. British Museum.

strained the resources of the largest modern construction-company.

Darius wanted to build a showplace, a focal point for Persian pride, a structure that would awe the rest of the empire. He also wanted it to be a kind of retreat, not to be used for the usual royal business. It would be primarily for Persians. None of the normal administrators or diplomats of the empire would set foot in it.

He chose a site farther south than any other royal residence, in a warmer climate than most, yet in the lee of the mountains, fifty-eight hundred feet above sea level, so that it would be pleasantly cool in the spring. It was off the normal traveling routes. He called the place Parsa, the name of his native land. The Greeks called it Persai and a Greek writer later deliberately corrupted it to Perseptolis (literally, "destroyer of cities"). From this finally came Persepolis.

Darius' unknown architects chose a rock shelf on the west side of the mountain. Then masses of forced slave labor went to work. No one will ever know how much human energy and anguish went into the creation of this place. Workers cleared and leveled the terrace, a space 1,500 by 900 feet of solid rock, hacking away the high places with no tools other than pick or hammer and wedge, filling holes with rubble.

They also began laying the west wall, facing the valley. Blocks of grayish limestone, some of it quarried near Pasargadae, were floated downriver on rafts and then hauled to the site on ox-drawn sleds. Each block was cut and smoothed with hammer, chisel, and file. The stonemasons probably had plumb bobs, levels, squares, and rod-and-string devices (which older civilizations had known for centuries) to help square off the stones. But it must have taken days to dress a single block, and some blocks weighed twenty tons.

Then the massive limestone chunks were pushed and pulled by man and beast, perhaps up slanting man-made inclines of earth or timber, to each course of stone. Probably they were

This magnificent set of stairs leads up the reception hall at Persepolis. In the background is the palace of Darius I, which dates to 522–486 B.C. Oriental Institute, University of Chicago.

inched and wiggled into place with the aid of levers. The stone blocks were not mortared, but the top row was securely anchored with a series of iron clamps — shaped like an hourglass and set in lead — dovetailed into the stone at every joint.

Two sets of stairs sprang up from ground level at the west side of the terrace, facing the valley. Midway up the side the stairs reversed direction, coming back together again at terrace level, some forty-five feet above ground. Each stairway had 111 steps of gray limestone polished slick as marble. Each step was twenty-three inches wide, with an easy four-inch rise, so that even horses and chariots could use them.

The Persepolis workmen, probably the same conscripts who

Gateway to the palace at Susa is marked by two statues of kings erected as monuments to themselves. Originally finished with glazed brick, statues, walls, hallways were a riot of glorious color. British Museum.

worked on the palace at Susa, built a drainage system and a cistern back at the edge of the mountain to catch fresh water. They carved enormous fluted-columns of wood or of "drums" of stone piled atop one another. These columns were probably raised with chains and bronze pulleys, which were found on the site, and with the aid of scaffolding, long used by the Egyptians. No mortar fastened the stone drums together; their sheer weight held them in place. However, the workmen laid the 12-by-12-by-15-inch mud-bricks in mud mortar, then faced them with greenish-gray mud plaster.

Roofs, a mixture of mud and straw laid on matting or branches over a frame or pole, had to be tramped firm. Some were then topped with decorative tiles and, on the ceiling side, lined with panels of imported wood.

Artists finished off the walls with ornate designs in glazed brick, relief carvings, or inscriptions. There were images of kings, tribute bearers, animals, and of course Ahura Mazda, a glorious sight in turquoise, scarlet, orange, deep purple, lapis lazuli blue, and touches of emerald green. Doorsills were of baked brick or polished stone. Doorways were edged in blue and scarlet. Wooden columns were plaster coated and painted red, blue, and white.

For those workmen the job seemed never to end. Indeed, it did not end in the lifetime of many. But as soon as the terrace, the apadana, and the first palace were complete, Darius began holding his annual New Year's Day reception at Persepolis. It was the great feast day of the year, a time for lavish gift-giving. It was always March 21 or 22, the vernal equinox—still the Iranian New Year and major holiday. And so vivid and complete are the carvings and the clay-tablet records that we can now reconstruct that festive scene in all its splendor.

The little town in the valley beneath Persepolis is dotted with tents, gay with pennants, and buzzing with voices. There is the barking of dogs and the neighing of horses. Delegates from all over the empire are marshaling to go up the hill and pay tribute to their king. It is a proud yet uneasy day for some of them. On the one hand, it is a rare honor to be allowed inside Persepolis. But the visitors are keenly aware that should their tributes fall short of what the king expects, they'll be lucky to get away with whole skins.

The foreign delegates trudge solemnly toward the vast terrace. It looks all the more formidable with its mud-brick walls sprinkled with guard towers, bringing the total height to some sixty feet. They fall into place behind certain senior members of the procession, ready to climb the double stairways. Even the stairs

An archaeological party excavates well site just east of palace at Persepolis. Here was an intricate underground water system which supplied the entire palace complex. Oriental Institute, University of Chicago.

are intimidating, polished to a high shine by hundreds of laborers with powder and rubbing-stones.

Outside at the stair entrances, inside at every key position, are guards: Persians and Medes stiffly at attention with spear butts at rest on the toe of the advanced right foot. Each wears a decorative ring in his left ear.

The procession begins, each little group preceded by an usher in metal collar, carrying a knobbed staff. First come the royal grooms, with whips and folded rugs.  One bears the royal foot-stool that the king uses for stepping into his chariot or when transferring from chariot to a more comfortable wagon.  Except in dire necessity, the royal foot never steps on common earth. Behind come grooms leading three of the king's famed Nesaean stallions.  All of this is strictly for show today, because Darius is already waiting upstairs and will not be using his chariot.

Now come two horse-drawn chariots, the wooden wheels studded with nails, the axle held to wheels with pins in the form of nude dwarfs.  There is a thong to help the monarch climb up and a metal handgrip to enable him to stand straight and majestic during the bone-shaking ride.  The white stallions are harnessed in gold-mounted bridles, painful gold bits, and orna-mented chestbands.  Their forelocks are tufted like lotus blos-soms and their manes are clipped into crests.

At last, the dignitaries arrive!  Here are thirty-two Persian and Median courtiers, relaxed and enjoying themselves.  Their beards are shorter than the king's but longer than those of lesser men.  The Persians wear fluted hats, robes, shoes with three straps, a dagger at the belt.  The Medes are in beribboned round hats, belted coats, trousers, laced shoes.  They wear a short sword at the hip and jangle with earrings and bracelets.  Some carry bow cases.  Nearly everyone has a flower as part of the festival.

As the privileged members of the empire, they have little fear of incurring the king's anger.  So, they behave as they would normally.  Some are pompous and haughty, consumed by their own self-esteem.  Some gossip with their neighbors.  Others touch their curled beards to assure themselves that every hair is in place.  Old men wheeze and strain.  One prankster tugs an-other man's beard.

Behind march the nervous delegates from the satrapies, twenty-three sets of them, providing a roll call of the empire. All are robed in their own fashion.  All include ornaments among their gifts, plus specialties of their region.

The Medes bring more of their splendid horses, of course. There are fine stallions, too, from Armenia and Cappadocia (part of modern Turkey), from Sagartia (now part of Iran) and Sogdiana (in the U.S.S.R.). The Syrians bring horses and chariots. The Libyans bring horses, chariots, and antelopes. From Parsa, Arachosia and, naturally, Bactria come two-humped Bactrian camels. The Egyptians, Gandarians (modern Russia), Babylonians, and Drangians (modern Iran) are leading bulls up the stairs. India is presenting jackasses and Arabia has dromedaries.

There is a snarling lioness on a rope, followed by her cubs, and two rams on a leash. And the Ethiopians, magnificent black men in sandals and ankle-length skirts, have brought an African mammal, the okapi, and a set of elephant tusks.

They reach the top of the stairs. Were this visit later, in the reign of Darius' son Xerxes, the visitors would file through a huge gatehouse, eighty feet square with a roof fifty-three feet high held up by four stone columns, the entrances guarded by colossal stone bulls, twenty-two feet high. They would pass through enormous double doors with metal facing and out again through another set.

As it is, they now turn right and approach the apadana. Like other major buildings on the terrace, it is on a raised platform, so the visitors climb more stairs and pause before the mightiest structure in all Persepolis. On three sides are porticoes, each roof held up by a dozen columns. The building proper is an enormous hall, about 600 feet square, with a forest of thirty-six columns seven feet in diameter and sixty-five feet high supporting roof beams of fragrant Lebanon cedar. The walls, seventeen feet thick, are of greenish-gray plaster laid on sun-dried mud-bricks. Here and there is an ornamental design made with glazed brick (rosette designs in green, yellow, and blue) or bits of gold.

Enter the king of kings! His bearers carry him in on the gold-plated throne and raise canopies over him. He wears a bejeweled golden crown and garments glittering with gold. He holds the

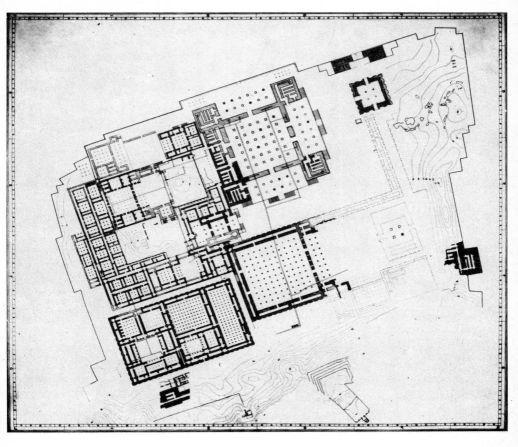

Ground plan of the palace at Persepolis. Light, wavy lines around perimeter denote terraces by which palace proper was approached. Large spaces represent the assembly halls studded by tiny squares indicating pillars which hold up the roof. Other squares adjoining are quarters of concubines. Oriental Institute, University of Chicago.

golden scepter in one hand. Two attendants follow, shielding the royal head with a golden parasol and swishing away flies with a whisk. A napkin or towel is ready, on one servant's arm, to mop the royal brow.

One by one the nobles present themselves. They bow low to his majesty while kissing a hand in his direction. The foreign

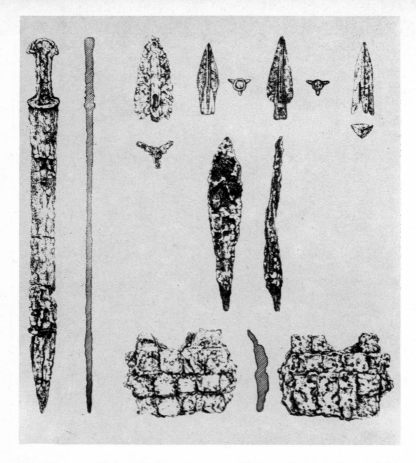

Many bronze objects including daggers and knives of curious shapes (left); arrowheads and blades for spears were recovered by sifting rubble at the ruins of Persepolis. Oriental Institute, University of Chicago.

visitors offer their tribute, prostrating themselves at the royal feet. Court attendants whisk the gifts away. Praise Ahura Mazda! The king is pleased!

While Darius accepts the tribute, servants file in and out of his palace behind the apadana—a great hall and four apartments—preparing the banquet. They are laden with cooked food kept warm in covered dishes, rare wines in bowls, and lesser wines in skin containers. Every day this court uses up literally thousands of animals and birds. The royal menu includes horses, camels, oxen, asses, deer, mutton, ostrich, geese, and chickens. The king gives several "wine banquets" during the year. The biggest is his own birthday party, when he entertains as many as fifteen thousand subjects, presents gifts to all, and runs up a bill of four hundred talents—about a half million dollars.

Yet he never really dines with his subjects. Today most of them—the representatives from subject lands—sit in the great hall while the king and a select few, probably Medes and Persians, dine apart. Even so, he takes his meal behind a white, green, and blue curtain, where he can see but not be seen.

The royal wives stay in the harem, surrounded by guardrooms full of eunuchs. They live somewhat less elegantly, for after all, they are not equals. So they occupy tiers of apartments, each apartment with a tiny hall and a little slot of a bedroom. (Although they did not participate in these ceremonies, the queens were often a power in palace politics.)

After Darius has dined from vessels of gold and silver, he invites the nobles to sit around and drink with him. They squat on the blue, white, black, and red paving stones while Darius stretches out on a couch with golden legs. The official wine-taster checks the wine to be sure no would-be assassin has poisoned it. Then Darius sips from a golden goblet. His wine is imported from sunny hills near Damascus. The nobles get a lesser vintage but still infinitely better than the common people even dream of tasting. Leftover food is passed out to the soldiers, slaves, and attendants. And finally, as the day wears on, the king, perhaps after a visit to the nearby harem, becomes thoroughly tipsy and is helped to his bed by the royal chamberlain. New Year's Day is over.

But the construction of Persepolis went on and on. In his lifetime Darius added the treasury and council hall. The treasury, like the harem, was expanded steadily as successive kings added to their collection of women and loot. It grew to 440 by 245 feet, 37 feet high, with a thicket of interior columns supporting the roof, and nearly 100 partitioned rooms. Here

Detail from bas relief, stairway wall, Persepolis, in which emmissaries from conquered people file past in endless succession bearing gifts as tribute to the king. British Museum.

the ivory, jewels, frankincense, carpets, clothes, weapons, spices, silver, and gold—most of it pillaged from conquered lands—piled up over the centuries.

Four other palaces were added over the years, including an elegant home for Xerxes. He, like Darius, loved pomp. He even built a throne hall with 100 columns—totally unnecessary because it fulfilled the same function as the apadana.

Today Persepolis is a strange half-shattered ghost. Many of the columns and gateposts stand again, stark white in the shadow of the mountain. Rebuilt, the harem looks much as it did in Darius' time. The outlines of the other buildings are clearly visible. The terrace is free ˃ rubble and the great stairs and relief drawings are more or less intact. Those parts that were of stone have survived the ravages of conquerors and centuries. "I built it secure and beautiful and adequate," Darius wrote of Persepolis. And so he did.

chapter 9

INSTANT ART

THE Greek artist hated
what he was doing. Here he was in Persepolis, far from home,
forced by Darius' overseers to carve flat, stiff likenesses of kings
and courtiers on Persian walls and stairways. There was no
depth, no extra fold in the tunic as it fell across the hip, no
emotion, little warmth in these stone-wall people set in their
ordered ranks. He longed to do a human finger on a human
hand, the way he felt a human hand and finger really looked.
Yet his Persian masters insisted on this style.

His fingers itched to do it his way. No one was looking. . . .
He seized a stylus. Swiftly but surely he sketched some heads
of bearded men, vivid and lifelike. He drew them right on the
side of the massive foot of one of the huge carved Persian figures!

Suddenly an overseer, the Persian master artist, drew near
to make sure the foreign artists were hard at work and doing
things the Persian way. Quickly the Greek covered his sketch
with the red paint that he was supposed to be applying to the
image. But he felt good. For a few seconds he had been able
to express himself in his own way.

Evidence uncovered centuries later has confirmed that this
incident — or something very much like it — actually happened.

Procession of satraps bringing presents as homage was a favorite theme of Persian artists. British Museum.

The hasty sketch of bearded faces was found by Ernst Herzfeld on a figure at Persepolis, its red paint weathered away by the centuries. The heads were almost identical with those found on Grecian vases of 510–500 B.C. We can well imagine that this anonymous Greek, like other subject artists raised in a different tradition, must have cringed at the kind of work demanded by the Persians. Yet such artists were brought from all over the empire and put to work, to create on demand, in a prescribed style and on a grand scale, the imperial art of the Achaemenids.

By the time of Darius the Medes and Persians were still newcomers to imperial power and literate civilization. As recently as forty years earlier they had not had the time, resources, or inclination to create a monumental art. They had been too busy fighting—fighting each other, outsiders, and the elements.

Now, for the first time, the empire was theirs to enjoy. They had conditions conducive to the creation of art on a grand scale, but their own artistic tradition was limited. True, as minor Median princes they had built columned audience halls in their seventh-century palaces. They had constructed massive forts to repel the Assyrian invaders. They had turned fine ceramics on the potter's wheel. They had exercised their native talent for

Death grapple between a lion and a bull from the capital of a pillar at Persepolis. Subject was a common one but the exercise of great freedom and imagination by the artist gives it meaning. British Museum.

casting in bronze and fashioning in gold almost all of the animals in the real world, as well as many beasts they saw only in their wildest imaginations. And they had learned how easy it was to borrow and enjoy the art of others. But they had never before built, decorated, and created in imperial dimensions.

Now they were eager to set fine tables, to bedeck their women with jewels, to construct great palaces, to adorn those palaces with reliefs; in short, to produce an art that would rival the greatest seen in the old worlds they had conquered. They were determined to have it. And so they decided to organize art, the way they organized everything else: a kind of instant art on the grand scale.

The end product was, naturally, a meld of elements borrowed from other cultures within the empire and of native Iranian traditions.   But whatever it was, the Medes and Persians put their own stamp on it.   Although the art historian today can walk the halls of Pasargadae or tramp the platform at Persepolis and pick out almost all the various elements that went into this art — a bit of Assyria here in the great bulls that guard the gate of Xerxes, something Egyptian there in the lintels over the windows of Darius' private palace, a suggestively Greek fold on one of the reliefs — the whole is not Assyrian, not Egyptian, not Greek. It is Persian.

Had the Achaemenids been without taste, they could have created an ornate hodgepodge, an artistic horror.   Instead, they brought into being one of the great art traditions of the world. It was an art that was regal, whether seen in the great audience hall of the king or the gold bracelet worn by his queen.   It was an art that made much of decoration for decoration's sake.   At times it lacked warmth and naturalness, but it was an art that caught and held the eye.

Nowhere are these characteristics better seen than in  Achaemenid architecture.   The central element in almost all of the great buildings at Susa, Pasargadae, and Persepolis was the columned hall.   This was their own.   Its history can be traced back in the archaeological record of the Iranian plateau to at least 1000 B.C.   By early Median times, before Cyaxares marched against the Assyrians, it had pretty much developed into the form in which we find it in the Achaemenid world.

In the rough old days when the Medes were a weak people, columned halls had been built with **walls** made entirely of mud-brick, and door and window frames of wood.   Columns at that time were nothing more than straight poplar tree-trunks set on uncut-stone bases.   How little such a building resembles the apadana at Persepolis, except in basic plan and concept.

Now windows and doors were of stone, with elaborate moldings done by "borrowed" Greek and Egyptian stonecutters.   The columns were massive fluted shafts of stone (possibly in the Greek manner), each set on a carefully shaped round base, ending in a highly decorative floral top, and capped by a "saddle" capital,

which was an Achaemenid touch. This capital was a double-headed beast—a bull, a griffin, or a lion. On the beast's back rode the massive wooden beam—probably of cedar from Lebanon and shaped by a Syrian carpenter—on which rested the cross-beams that held the roof.

In earlier, cruder times this capital had been nothing more than a forked top, shaped like a Y, on the upper end of a poplar trunk. That same technique can be seen in many of the country teahouses of Iran today, for the columned hall has remained typically Persian.

Finally, this massive columned-hall might be further decorated with the bas-relief work for which the Achaemenids were equally famous. Although such carvings might illustrate an incident (such as the subject peoples bringing tribute to the king in his palace), they did not tell narrative stories as did reliefs and wall paintings in Egypt. The object of Egyptian wall reliefs was to inform and entertain. Achaemenid reliefs were for purposes of decoration, to enhance the architecture, to increase one's sense of grandeur, to give people something to admire on the way into the palace, to awe the viewer with the imperial might of Persia.

Nor did Persian art, particularly in Darius' time, have much depth or three-dimensional effect. Unlike Greek reliefs, those at Persepolis are precise but flat. Animals are done with the most zest. The carved horses come alive—lips and nostrils flaring, bit and bridle carefully delineated. But people? The early Achaemenid artists seemed unable to render people realistically.

(Above) Gold fish and (right) intricate bronze pin both among treasures of Oxus are examples of Persian craftsmanship. British Museum.

The figures are never lifelike.   At times they are not even good flat work.   Some have no line marking wrist or knuckle, no attempt to differentiate between thumb and fingers.   (Fingers seem to have been a particular problem.)

Later, under Darius' son Xerxes, reliefs seem to have more style.   Some of the garments have a semblance of tucks where the belt circles the waist.   Clothes look a little more like clothes. They are carved in folds with zigzag edges, reflecting the form of the human body inside.   The thighs, in these later reliefs, no longer vary in length for the same figure.   Forms do not overlap; nor do people tread on one another's toes.   The comparative skills of individual sculptors actually begin to show, and reflect their individuality.   Here is one who understands the function of the curved line, and so has created graceful, mobile fingers. Here is an artist who carves skinny fingers, heads, and shoulders. A third produces squat, clumsy people with ungainly heads.

But early or late in the artistic tradition, what the Persians did best were things.   Like the fine bits and bridles, all the material things worn or carried by figures in the reliefs were carved with perfection and tremendous attention to detail.   The scabbard worn by a Median soldier on one relief at Persepolis is so delicately done that the beholder feels it must be real, is tempted to touch it, and is startled to find it cold stone instead of warm gold.

From their own ancestors the Achaemenids inherited a tradition of fine metalwork.   Hundreds of small exquisite bronze

Stylized head of bull from capital of column at Persepolis shows Assyrian influence in stiffness and formality of detail.  British Museum.

items have been dug from ancient graves in the province of Luristan, in the Zagros Mountains of western Iran:   pieces of harness,
bracelets, bowls, plaques, axes, belts, small figurines, daggers,
pendants, and pins, dating approximately to the seventh and
eighth centuries B.C.

By the Achaemenid period the Persians had brought goldsmiths and silversmiths from other lands to Iranian workshops.
These meticulous craftsmen did not come willingly, but they
were well paid for their labors.   They did their best on the things
their masters admired and understood, such things as wild and
domestic animals.   Here, a gold drinking cup in the form of a
winged lion; there, a silver ibex (a goat with long, backward-
curving horns) inlaid with gold.   Lions, bulls, dragons, cypress
trees, horses, mythical creatures — over and over they appear
on plaques and weapons and personal ornaments.

Even the smallest items of fine Achaemenid art have a monumental air about them.   It is almost as though whatever the
Persians touched in this period took on an imperial flavor.   The
same creative energies that went into politics and political organization also were channeled into art and artistic organization.

Take a latent native artistic-potential, basic good taste, and
a newly acquired imperial attitude; add access to the finest artists
in the entire Near East and almost unlimited resources in money
and labor; and stir in a little creative imagination.

The result:   Achaemenid art.

Imaginative figurine in
bronze of female goddess
was among many
intriguing statuettes re-
covered from Oxus.
Louvre.

chapter 10

ALL THE KING'S MEN

Down the Royal Road
they marched in clouds of dust — the soldiers of the king. It was
491 B.C. and the army was leaving Susa for yet another war, this
time with some rebellious Greeks. As always, the common
people of the empire lined the road to watch and wave. They
were not much interested in the war. There were always wars
going on somewhere. This one was far away, against seemingly
insignificant people. But the Persians always loved to see their
army march by. It was fine entertainment.

It took hours for Darius' army to pass. There were baggage
detachments with supplies and tents loaded on camels. There
were thousands of infantry and high-stepping cavalry.

In the very middle of these legions of men eight prancing white
horses drew the sacred chariot of Ahura Mazda, in which no man
ever sat. If the Wise Lord himself was in it, no one could see
him. Its driver trotted alongside on foot.

Behind that rode the senior man on earth, the king of kings,
and somewhere, trailing after, came Darius' private food supply.
Whole flocks of animals were herded along to provide the king
with fresh meat. Mule-drawn wagons hauled silver vessels

of boiled water from the Choaspes River, near Susa, for the king alone to drink.

All of this was wondrous, indeed, but what really stirred the onlookers, or at least all the capering small boys, was —

"There they are!   The Immortals!"

There was no mistaking the Ten Thousand Immortals, the elite corps of the Persian army.   The very name suggested romance and heroism.   If one man fell in battle, another hand-picked, superbly trained soldier would instantly be ready to take his place.   Thus there were always Ten Thousand Immortals.

They were Medes and Persians.   Some of them were swarthy, some were fair, but they immediately stood out among the other troops.   A thousand of them acted as the king's personal body-guard.   They were fiercely loyal and ready to fight to the death for him.   Each carried a spear of cornel wood (of the dogwood family and very hard), with a glittering silver blade and a distinctive golden pomegranate on the handle.   The other nine thousand bore spears adorned with silver pomegranates.

A bow and quiver of arrows hung from every man's left shoulder, the quiver decorated in strips and crescents of blue, brown, or yellow leather.   Their robes flowed to their wrists and ankles, sometimes in light purple or yellow, sometimes trimmed with yel-

**Bronze statuette of horseman represents one of the Immortals (archers on horseback) who guarded the safety of the king.**

low and brown stars or squares. They wore blue or yellow shoes of soft leather, laced or buttoned. A twist of green cord held back their hair, gathered in a bun at the back. Their short beards were tightly curled. Gold earrings and gold bracelets glittered from heads and wrists.

We know from the Persepolis reliefs and the glazed-brick decorations of Susa just how the Immortals looked, just as we know many other things about the king's army. The army held the empire together. Enlightened though some Achaemenid kings were, they ruled primarily by force. They could never have held the far-flung conquered lands together without a strong army. Furthermore, being a soldier was one of the best kinds of life for a man. After all, was not Darius himself a fighting man?

"Inasmuch as my body has the strength, as battlefighter I am a good battlefighter," Darius said, in the autobiography that was distributed throughout his empire. "Trained am I both with hands and with feet. As a horseman I am a good horseman. As a bowman I am a good bowman, both afoot and on horseback. As a spearman I am a good spearman, both afoot and on horse-back. . . . O menial, vigorously make thou known of what sort I am, and of what sort my skillfulnesses and of what sort my superiority . . ."

For once Darius was probably not exaggerating. He was a peerless soldier. He rose to power as a vigorous young man who had personally headed the Immortals in Cambyses' day. He had won the throne with his sword as well as his wits. He understood the military as he understood most other things.

His army, like everything else he touched, was perfectly organized. At its peak it may have totaled 360,000 men. It was arranged by tens: 10,000 men to a division, broken down into battalions, companies, and squads of 1,000, 100, and 10 men, respectively. There was a parallel breakdown according to type: lancers, archers, and cavalry.

Yet, also in the Persian manner, Darius permitted his subjects a certain individuality in dress and weapons. For the most part this was common sense. In those days it would have been impossible to fit thousands of men with identical uniforms.

Yet it probably pleased the men of other nations in his army to be able to fight in their national dress. A Persian army on the march was an astonishing sight, a sort of walking encyclopedia of the empire. So widely assorted were the outfits that it must have been difficult to tell friend from foe.

There were helmets of bronze, wood, leather, and woven wicker; helmets bedecked with the horns and the ears of oxen. There were plumed hats and foxskin headdresses. And there were leather jackets, gaily dyed cloaks, goatskins, crimson leggings, fawnskin boots, and Arabian flowing robes. The Ethiopians were especially magnificent, their dark bodies smeared with chalk and vermilion and draped in lion or leopard skins.

The pomp, majesty and absence of any lifelike quality in the rendering of this warrior figure are characteristic of Persian art. From a relief on the walls at Persepolis.

A horse's bit is made decorative by adding these two bronze figures of the ibex although they serve no useful purpose. British Museum.

Some men were armed with spears, javelins, daggers, battle-axes, or clubs studded with iron. The Indians carried cane bows and iron-tipped cane arrows. The Ethiopians were walking arsenals with six-foot spears made from palm ribs, stone-tipped arrows, other spears tipped with sharpened antelope-horns, and knobby clubs.

If the dress and weapons alone did not send shivers up an enemy's spine, the mode of attack did. An enemy never knew exactly how an Achaemenid company might charge. The Iranians rode horses; the Libyans attacked in chariots; the Arabs loped into battle on camels. And the nomad Sagartians (from what is now central Iran) carried daggers and rawhide lassos. Their trick was to rope an enemy like a rodeo steer, reel him in, and stab him before he could struggle free.

What was it like to be one of the king's men? For those ordinary subjects from other lands it was a good enough life. There were many worse ways to die, and while one lived, the living was good. The empire supported the army. A large part of every

Handle of dagger is richly chased with design of human head, perhaps a portrait of the owner. Believed to have been made early in the first century, B.C. British Museum.

year's taxes went for the upkeep of the troops. While we find no record of pay, the men may have received a modest cash allowance plus food and clothing. The food was simple, with barley bread as the staple, but a soldier could always count on eating regularly.

On campaigns, the countries that the army passed through had to support the troops. A soldier might take a sheep, a goatskin of wine, or even a woman, and the ordinary citizen dared not protest.

But for a Mede or a Persian a position of leadership in the army was the noblest career a man could follow. These men were the backbone of the army, reflecting their mountainfighter heritage. They were still the only people Darius could really trust. The son of every leading Persian was trained at the nearest court or satrapal city in the solid values of old-fashioned Persian life, which included simple diet, hard riding, hunting, and skill with the bow. In every city or other strategic point throughout the empire, Persians manned the garrisons. Senior officers nearly everywhere were Persians, generally members of the leading families.

And every Mede or Persian could aspire to becoming an Immortal someday. That was the best life. Although the regular garrison of Immortals at Persepolis, for example, did not live in luxury, existence was comfortable by the standards of the day. The men occupied small rooms in a mud-brick building that was back out of sight on the terrace, near the base of the mountain. The sanitary arrangements were crude: little brick sewers led directly into the barracks' street. We know the floors indoors were rarely swept because their level rose steadily with the accumulated rubble of the years. There evidently was little or no furniture. The Immortals must have slept on the floor and piled their splendid armor in a corner.

But they dined well on leftovers from the king's table, and they had plenty to drink. In their quarters archaeologists found many kinds of pottery: flat canteens for long rides and battles, bowls

Picture of horse on side, plus extra handle of unusual length indicate this vase may have been made for particular use of horsemen. British Museum.

with spouts that shot liquid straight into the drinker's mouth, pitchers, low jugs, and tall, slender wine jars with pointed bases that could be stuck directly into the earthen floor.

On campaigns abroad the Immortals were given special privileges. They carried their own food supply, better than the average soldier's. Wives or concubines — the so-called camp followers — were allowed to travel with them.

So the army lived satisfactorily in peacetime, died for what they believed was a noble cause in wartime, and to a large extent provided the glue that held the realm together. Even in the last crumbling years of the empire the army, so well constructed by Darius, remained sound while other facets of society did not, and so kept the facade of the empire intact. Much of what the Achaemenids left to the world was made possible by the soldiers of the king.

chapter

# A CRACK IN THE EMPIRE

ON the evening of September 11, 491 B.C., a lean, muscular man named Philippides, who had been trained as a professional runner, jogged swiftly out from the city of Athens in the republic of Attica. He was bound for Sparta in the neighboring republic of Laconia. Philippides measured his pace, for he was racing against time, and for the survival of his people. Darius, king of Persia, and his powerful army had just landed on the shores of what is now Greece (then a collection of several small countries or city-states). Athens desperately needed Sparta's help.

Philippides made the trip of 150 miles over winding, rocky, hilly trails in forty-eight hours, an average of three miles an hour —an incredible feat. It matters little, in retrospect, that the Spartans refused to respond to his plea for help. (They were celebrating a religious festival that culminated with the full moon, nearly two weeks away, and sacred custom forbade them to fight.) That run, the first "marathon race," was forever preserved in history. It was linked to one of the glorious moments of all time: the battle of Marathon, where little Greece met the mighty Achaemenid Empire head on.

The disputes leading to that battle had been simmering for years.  The people we now know as Greeks had begun settling on the east and west shores of the Aegean Sea many centuries before the Achaemenids rose to power.  Although they battled among themselves and set up independent states, their dialects were rooted in one language, and ethnically, they were all cousins.

By the late sixth century B.C. most of the Greek city-states were newly linked together in the Peloponnesian League.  The league was a move toward joint protection.  Members were not bound to one another but each had a mutual-aid agreement with Sparta, for the fierce, valiant Spartans were the supreme warriors of the group.

So far, these people in what is now Greece proper had escaped Persian conquest.  The Aegean Sea was a partial buffer-zone,

(Left) Head of a bull, (right) figure of a boy were both done in silver. Bull's head was probably the fragment of a handle, the boy, a statuette. British Museum.

and also, other conquests had kept the Achaemenids busy. But the Greek-speaking Ionians, who lived across the Aegean on the eastern shore (now part of western Turkey), had long ago fallen captive, first to the Lydians and then to the Achaemenids.

By 499 B.C. Ionia had had enough of the Persians' choice of local tyrants and their perennial drain on Greek purses. The Ionians rose in rebellion and looked across the Aegean for help. Athens sent a few shiploads of men. The Grecian allies marched on Sardis, the one-time Lydian capital, and burned it to the ground.

On the way back to the Aegean coast, however, a Persian army intercepted and defeated the allies. The Athenians promptly fled for home and helped no more in the Ionian revolt. But Athens had already made an enemy of the powerful Achaemenid king. Herodotus writes that Darius, upon hearing of the burning of Sardis, asked, "The Athenians? Who are they?" Upon finding out, he allegedly told one of his slaves to say to him three times at dinner, "Sire, remember the Athenians." Darius did.

Lacking support from the free Grecian states, the Ionian revolt flickered feebly on. Finally, in 494, Darius got around to teaching the rebels a lesson. He dispatched an army and six hundred ships to Miletus, the principal Ionian city on the Aegean.

The Ionians fought gallantly but in vain. The Persians stormed through the city, committing a series of atrocities that were ferocious even for those times. The seaboard quarter of Miletus was leveled so completely that for decades after, it was not rebuilt. The temple was burned. Most of the men were butchered. Women and children were shipped to Mesopotamia. Darius, to his credit, was not personally on hand. When he heard about the savagery, he ordered it stopped. Then he returned to the Ionians a semblance of democratic government.

But, though he thought he had been putting down a rebellion, Darius had actually been stirring up a hornet's nest. The Athenians, who had given so little support to the revolt, now grew emotional and belligerent.

Darius' excellent communications network soon picked up word of Athenian hostility.  He had not forgotten how Athens had helped Ionia.  An aroused Athens might stir that country to act again.  Athens had to be disciplined as an example to other potential troublemakers in that part of the world.

In 491 a Persian army sailed across the Aegean, up a narrow channel separating the island state of Euboea from Attica.  They landed and laid siege to Euboea's leading city, Eretria.  The Persian force, by conservative estimates, totaled 25,000 infantry and 1,000 cavalry.  Since Eretria could barely muster 3,000 foot soldiers and 600 horsemen, to meet the Persians on a battlefield would be suicide.  The Eretrians barricaded themselves inside their city and sent a plea to Athens for help.

It was at that moment that Philippides set out for Sparta.  If the Persians were to be stopped, all the Grecian states would have to act in concert.  Athens at once dispatched its army of 10,000 heavily armed *hoplites* (spearmen) and some lighter-armed troops toward Euboea.  They headed for the Attic town of Chalcis, at the narrowest neck of the channel, a mere stone's throw across the water from Euboea.  There the little Athenian navy, squeezed like a cork into the neck of a bottle, might be able to hold the Persian fleet at bay long enough for Athens' army to be ferried across.

The king seated upon his throne appears in one of the capitals of a pillar in the great audience hall. This was another favorite theme of Persian artists. British Museum.

But even as the Athenians marched, a runner brought alarming news. Part of the Persian force, some 15,000 infantrymen, had landed at Marathon, on Attica itself. The Athenians changed course and started for Marathon. Only then did they find out how badly they were outnumbered. They hesitated. Then came more tragic news: Eretria had been burned and its people deported.

Attica was alone now and fighting for its life. Worse than that, the other wing of Darius' army, with Eretria wiped out, was free to sail to loot undefended Athens. This was bound to happen unless the Persian force could be smashed at Marathon.

The plain of Marathon, some twenty air miles from Athens, curves like a half-moon along the shoreline, backed by a chain of hills. The Athenian general Miltiades, a brilliant strategist, moved his men into a small valley commanding the only two roads leading from the plain to the capital. There they waited. The longer they delayed, the more their hopes grew that help from Sparta would come in time. They were further heartened by the fact that a thousand men from friendly Plataea, in the near-by state of Boeotia, appeared to fight alongside the Athenians.

Days passed. The Persians grew uneasy. Finally they sent one war party toward Athens by ship. The main army rose up on September 21. They would march right over those upstart Greeks in the mountains and take Athens by land and sea.

The armies moved toward one another — mass of men tramping toward mass of men — with the clank of armor, the ominous scrape of swords being drawn from scabbards, the glitter of spears in morning sun, the rustle of arrows moving from quiver to bow-string. It was that breathtaking strangely quiet instant on the verge of every ancient battle, just before the mass slaughter.

Suddenly at two hundred yards, as the Persians were tightening their bowstrings, the hoplites let out a roar and charged at the double. They came at a speed unheard of among heavily armored foot soldiers. Their onslaught caught the Persians completely by surprise. The Greeks broke through the rain of

Persian arrows and suddenly were on top of the Persian archers. At close range the spear-thrusting hoplite, with huge metal shield and a helmet that covered his entire head except for his eyes and mouth, was a sight to chill the blood.

Even so, after the first shock the Persians rallied. The Greek center sagged back, back, back, before the thrust of the Immortals. But there were less-valiant members of the Achaemenid army in the left and right wings, and they were driven back to the sea. At that moment the Greeks whirled, entrapped the Persian center from the rear, and tore it to bits.

Some of the Achaemenids broke and fled for their ships. The Greeks hunted them down, killing them in the shallows and at the sides of their ships. They even managed to burn seven of the enemy vessels. By noon the fight was over. There were 6,400 Persians dead or dying on the bloody field. The Greek forces had lost 192 men.

When the Persian naval squadron dropped anchor off Athens, they were startled to find themselves facing the Athenian army which had hurried home from the battle of Marathon. The Persians looked, and hesitated. The news of Marathon, the sight of the Greeks grimly prepared for another fight, plus the fact that 2,000 Spartans were on the march at last, was too much bad news for the Persian commander. The fleet hoisted sail and fled.

For Darius, Marathon was little more than a mosquito bite, a small, annoying loss of prestige. From an army so vast he could afford the loss of manpower. He swore he would teach the Greeks a thorough lesson, however, as soon as he could get around to it.

But he never did. Campaigns were slow to mount and move in ancient times. Five years later, before he could even the score with Greece, Darius died. His successor was not up to the task, and the Greeks had grown even tougher. They had a tradition to live up to, now. So the gallant stand at Marathon, by itself a small thing in the sweep of history, turned out to be the first fissure in the crumbling structure of the Persian Empire.

(Above) One of the many necklaces fashioned with great artistry in the Oxus collection. (Left) Massive gold bracelet embellished with two symmetrically-balanced griffons is considered the prize of the collection. British Museum.

## chapter 12

XERXES—A PERSIAN TRAGEDY

IT is 486 B.C., in the reign of Xerxes. The satrap of Media has been granted an audience with this new king of kings. For splendor and ceremony he has never seen a sight to equal this one at Persepolis.

He stands well back, and subservient, while Xerxes, the thirty-five-year-old son of Darius, enters the apadana. Xerxes' face is arresting: prominent eyes, slightly curved nose, drooping moustache twisted at the ends, a king's distinctive square-cut beard with its precise rows of curls. His outer robe is worth a huge fortune: twelve thousand talents, they say. Is it possible? Probably, for it is dyed in precious Phoenician purple and thickly embroidered with fighting-hawk designs in pure gold thread. Beneath it is a purple garment with white spots. Such a garment can be worn by no other man in the empire. White trousers with purple cuffs are visible beneath the robe, over pointed blue shoes.

Gold bracelets and a gold collar gleam as he steps with measured tread toward his throne. From the gold waistband swings a short Persian sword; its entire sheath, they say, is made from a single precious stone. In his right hand he holds the slender,

Winged lion with human head, reminiscent of Egyptian sphinx, guards Persepolis from top of stairway. British Museum.

knobbed gold scepter; in his left, a lotus flower with two buds, as is the custom with Achaemenid kings.

Xerxes eases himself into a cushioned throne made of wood encased in gold. Its gold lions' paw feet are set on balls of silver. Over his head is a canopy, inlaid with jewels, richly tasseled, and supported by gold pillars. Xerxes rests one foot on the royal footstool. He extends his scepter to indicate that the visitor is recognized and does not displease him. Respectfully the satrap advances and bows deeply. All during the audience the visitor is required to keep his hands deep within his sleeves — for Xerxes fears assassins. Were the Mede suddenly to withdraw a hand, an Immortal from the bodyguard would cut him down.

Afterward, when the king of kings has departed, the visitor is permitted a lingering look at the throne, under the scowling eyes of the Immortals. Naturally, he must never lay a finger on it.

Such was the pomp of Xerxes, carefully pieced together by modern historians from scores of writings of the time. It is a significant facet of Achaemenid history. Every Persian ruler surrounded himself with an aura of elegance, but none loved splendor more than Xerxes.  It led to his undoing.  Xerxes, who might have been a great king, was to disintegrate in tragedy.

Xerxes, however, was not a total failure, in the manner of most of those who came after him.  He mounted the throne equipped with twelve years' experience as satrap of Babylon.  Some of his administrative measures were sound.  But it was under his rule that the country began its long decline.

The empire he inherited was basically sound.  It was troubled with inflation but reinforced with a magnificent army and still known for tolerant attitudes that satisfied most of its varied people.  Yet Xerxes was not an adequate caretaker.  He had no talent for economics.  He reveled too much in court pleasures and in the building of monuments and palaces (at which he excelled).  He was easily swayed by bad advisers and so drawn

Figure of a Persian king reproduced in form of a statuette.  British Museum.

into some disastrous wars. His treatment of subject peoples
was contrary to the Achaemenid tradition. His reign was noted
not for what it was, but for what it might have been; not for his
glory, but for the glory of his enemies.

Xerxes' first task on assuming the throne was to quell a revolt
in Egypt, which sprang up just before Darius' death. He
accomplished it, but without finesse. By January 484 Egypt
was back in the fold, although crushed and bleeding. Temple
property was confiscated; Egyptians were harshly treated.
Xerxes, unlike earlier Achaemenids, made no attempt to con-
ciliate the conquered people by the pretense of being a "native"
king.

Meanwhile, in Babylonia, his rule had been happily accepted.
As satrap, he had governed well enough. But now, as king,
Xerxes bungled. To the traditional title "King of Babylon, King
of Lands," he added "King of Parsa and Mada." He did it,
apparently, to add grandeur to his title, but Babylonia took it
as a demotion and a threat. In view of Egypt's recent treatment, the Babylonians feared that they too might lose their institutions and their identity. They rose and killed their satrap,
Zopyrus—he who had once betrayed them to the Persians and
had been so well rewarded for his deed by Darius.

Xerxes knew only one kind of response: force. He ordered
his ranking general, Megabyzus, to bring Babylonia to heel.
The troops smashed fortifications and temples alike. They
melted down an eight-hundred-pound gold statue of the god
Bel Marduk and killed the priests who protested. Babylonian
estates were confiscated and handed over to Persians. Babylon
was almost wiped out. Many of its records were destroyed.
Syria was detached from Babylonia and made a separate satrapy.
Babylonia became part of Assyria. From that time on, surviving
Babylonians were taxed more relentlessly than ever.

Over and over through his twenty-one-year reign Xerxes let
his undisciplined temper run riot. The Greek city-states were
still agitating. From Persia's standpoint, Marathon was not yet

avenged.    Urged on by ambitious courtiers, Xerxes launched
an assault by land and sea.    His objective was nothing less than
the annihilation of Greece.

Xerxes chose to move his army by land all the way to Greece,
rather than to cross the Aegean.    This meant marching through
what is now Turkey, up the east and north shores of the Aegean,
and into what is now northern Greece.    The fleet would sail
at his elbow all the way.

Such a plan required massive advance preparations.    Great
stockpiles of corn and other supplies were set up en route.    At
one point, to avoid sending the fleet around a dangerous promontory, Xerxes ordered the digging of a canal a mile and a half long.
It took laborers, driven by whips, three years to dig the channel.

On the way to Sardis for the winter of 481–480 the king and
his army were entertained by Pythius, a rich Lydian.    Not only
did Pythius wine and dine them, he offered to donate 3,993,000
gold darics to the war cause.    Xerxes was so overcome with grati-
tude (not many people voluntarily offered him money) that he
instead gave Pythius 7,000 darics to round out his fortune.

Then Pythius pressed his luck.    He asked a favor: Would the
king spare Pythius' eldest son from military service?    In a flash
Xerxes' good humor turned to rage.    How dare this "slave" make
such a request when the king himself was marching off to battle
(albeit marching deep and fairly safely in the center of a very large
army)?    Pythius' son was forthwith cut in two.    Half of his body
was displayed on either side of the gate of Sardis as the troops
marched out—a warning to anyone else who might consider
asking a royal favor.

The Persians drew up at the Hellespont (now the Dardanelles).
Phoenician and Egyptian engineers had built a bridge across it,
but violent storms had shattered their handiwork.    Xerxes in-
dulged in another rage.    He had the engineers' heads cut off and
ordered three hundred lashes for the waters of the Hellespont.
(Modern psychiatrists would have found Xerxes a fascinating
study.)

His men, presumably keeping straight faces at the risk of losing their heads, obediently whipped the waves, while chanting, "O bitter water, our lord lays this punishment upon thee for having done him wrong, who never did wrong to thee. Xerxes the King will cross thee, whether thou wilt or not. Just is it that no man sacrifice to thee, for thou art a treacherous and briny river."

The royal megalomaniac then set a fresh squad of engineers to building a double bridge. This one was of wood and earth, built over 674 anchored *triremes* (ships with three rows of oars) and *penteconters* (ships with fifty oars). From high atop a marble throne on shore Xerxes watched it to completion. Then he reviewed his troops, ordered incense burned on the bridges, and prayed to the sunrise. Evidently having forgiven the Hellespont, he cast an offering of cup, sword, and bowl into the water and gave the marching orders.

The army crossed in a continuous two-day stream—stragglers being helped along by a smart flick of the whip. The baggage train followed, taking another five days to cross. The army moved into Greece, 180,000 men, with a fleet of 800 vessels keeping pace along the coasts. Xerxes slept in the only tent; his men lay under the stars or rain. Cities along the way were forced to feed the army at a cost of the equivalent of a half million dollars per day.

The Greeks fell back steadily before this multitude. The confident Persians seemed to be winning by default, but they continued to woo the gods. At one point, claims Herodotus, the Magi offered several white horses; later they sacrificed nine native children.

The Greeks, although retreating, were only looking for a favorable battleground. At last they chose one. It was a narrow pass between sea and mountains. Someday its name would be known to every schoolboy in the Western world. It was called Thermopylae. Today, because the sea has receded, the pass is hardly recognizable, but at that time it was narrow and the gateway to much of eastern Greece. There was only one way around it:

a rough, steep mountain trail that could lead an enemy to a position behind the defenders of Thermopylae.

Facing the Persians in the pass stood the Spartan king Leonidas with 7,000 men. The Greek fleet, 324 triremes and 9 penteconters, was anchored on the north coast of Euboea. The Persian navy pulled in off a neighboring coast. There were so many vessels that some ships had to form eight lines parallel to shore. A storm blew up and raged for twenty-four hours. Some of the Persian vessels were dashed to pieces on the coast. Others crashed into one another and sank.

Xerxes and his thousands found Thermopylae to be a formidable barrier. The king of kings paused and waited four days, perhaps hoping the enemy would flee in sheer awe at the sight of him. The Spartans were not that sort.

On the fifth day Xerxes attacked. The Spartan spearmen forced his archers back. A day later Xerxes tried again. Again the Spartans held. Even the Immortals, pride of all Persia, couldn't budge these ferocious defenders. Xerxes "sprang thrice from his throne in agony for his army," the chronicles tell us.

Led by a renegade Greek, a detachment of Immortals went over the secret back-trail. A party of mercenaries, guarding this route, took to their heels. The Persians closed in from the rear. Leonidas, the moment he learned that he was being surrounded, evacuated his main force. Perhaps he wanted to save his main army from massacre, while delaying Xerxes until, hopefully, the Greeks could win a naval battle that would change his fortunes.

The Persians attacked from the rear. Leonidas sent out one detachment to meet this danger. He and three hundred specially picked men faced the Persian army at the front of the pass. Rather than fight defensively, the Spartans charged the enemy. Leonidas fell and died, and a violent fight raged around his body. Two of Xerxes' brothers were slain in the same battle. Many Persians were driven into the sea or trampled by their retreating fellows.

Persian commanders forced their reluctant men back into the fight. At last the sheer mass of the empire overwhelmed the dwindling band of Spartans.  When the battle ended, not one Spartan survived.

Afterward the enraged Xerxes sent for Leonidas' body and ordered the head impaled on a stake for all to see.  It was an indignity to a brave foe that would have shamed Darius or Cyrus.

The Greek fleet pulled back and Xerxes marched on to Athens unhindered.  There a stubborn handful of defenders in the Acropolis (hilltop citadel) held out for two weeks, rolling stones down on the Persians.  But at last the invaders scaled the hill, cut down the defenders, plundered the temples, and set fire to everything that would burn.

Most of the Persian fleet—about three hundred fifty vessels— was holding the Greek navy bottled up in a sound between the island of Salamis and the mainland.  To make the situation additionally indefensible for the Greeks, more Persian ships were on

Fanciful gold plaquettes combine human heads with winged bodies of griffons.  Heads are repeated along bottom row.  British Museum.

A Greek slave arrived in the Persian camp. He "revealed" that the Greeks planned to slip away in the night around the back of Salamis. If Xerxes struck now and destroyed them, hinted the slave, all Greek resistance would end.

That night Xerxes eagerly sent two hundred Egyptian ships around to the southern promontory of Salamis to block the "escape." He fell into the trap — for a trap it was — set by Themistocles, the Greek soldier-statesman, thus weakening the main force. In the morning, September 23, 480 B.C., Xerxes launched his attack. He watched it all from a high throne on the mainland, like a spectator at a football game.

At dawn the little ships rowed and sailed into the straits in three columns. The Greeks, who of course had never thought of retreating, darted out from behind a finger of land, lured the first Persian column in like a fish to the net, then closed around it. On the shores spectators cheered or cursed, depending on which side they were on. The large number of Persian ships was now a hindrance in the small area. They got in each other's way. More Persian vessels crowded into the strait. The Greeks charged them at neatly timed intervals, herding them into bunches like sheep, sometimes cutting enemy ships in half by ramming them with their own heavily reinforced prows.

One Persian ship, commanded by Artemisia, the fierce queen of the satrapy Caria, was so hotly pursued by a Greek that she had only one ruthless choice: She deliberately sank one of her own ships to provide herself an avenue of escape. Xerxes in his grandstand seat was told mistakenly that Artemisia had downed an enemy. "My men have become women, my women men," groaned the king.

He had, in fact, lost half his navy. The Persian survivors, fleeing from a floating rubble of wrecks, were clubbed like fish. Another brother of Xerxes died in battle.

Salamis, like Marathon years before, was more of a moral loss for the Persians than a dangerous defeat, but psychological failures had a profound effect on a king like Xerxes. He compounded his loss of face by lapsing into another rage and executing his Phoenician captains for cowardice. The rest of the Phoenicians, infuriated, promptly turned their backs and went home. The Egyptians soon followed their lead.

Winter was near. Xerxes rushed most of his navy ahead to the Hellespont to guard the bridge and line of retreat, leaving General Mardonius to hold the captured lands. At the Hellespont Xerxes found that fate had thwarted him again. The bridge was gone, perhaps destroyed by storms. He crossed by boat and wintered at Sardis, not far from the Aegean coast.

Even at this point Persia still could have saved the campaign. The capable Mardonius had a hand-picked corps of Immortals —Persians, Medes, Bactrians, and Indians—the cream of the army. In the spring, after vainly trying to placate the Greeks with offers of autonomy, alliance, and reparation, he went back to battle.

At Plataea, Persia again underestimated the sheer ferocity of Greeks fighting with their backs to the wall. Once more the Persians cornered the Spartans. Had the Persians permitted the Greeks to retreat, opposition probably would have disintegrated. Athens would have no doubt come to terms and other city-states might have capitulated. But Mardonius wanted to be sure—and victory looked so easy.

The Persians pressed forward behind a wall of wicker shields, showering arrows on the trapped Spartans. Then it was hand-to-hand combat, which the heavily armored Spartans loved and performed surpassingly well. Unlike most commanders, Mardonius on his white charger personally led rally after rally. It was a fatal mistake. A Spartan spearman brought him down, and without him, his army fell apart.

Almost simultaneously the Persian naval camp was invaded by the Greeks. The Persians, caught by surprise, were overwhelmed. Their ships were burned at anchor. Then, joined in confederation, the Grecian states won another massive naval victory on the north shore of the Mediterranean, not far from

Cyprus.  Now Persia stood stripped of its European possesssions outside Asia Minor.  What Darius had won, Xerxes had lost.

Discouraged and bitter, Xerxes gave up all attempts at conquest.  He spent his final days building and improving his glorious palaces.  Drained by years of crippling and useless war, his subjects were now milked of money and labor to complete these monuments to the royal vanity.

Xerxes derived scant pleasure from court life, however.  It was racked with intrigue, to which the king contributed his share. Eventually Xerxes had one of his brothers and his brother's sons murdered for plotting against him.  But this was merely the beginning of an era of decadence and palace scandal that was to last for five generations.  The harem quarters were enlarged yet always overcrowded.  The eunuchs who infested the court grew increasingly influential.  Bit by bit the commander of the royal guard, Artabanus, and his eunuch chamberlain, Aspamitres, gained sway over the king.

One night in 465 these two, aided by one of Xerxes' sons-in-law, murdered the king in his bedchamber.  Thus fell Xerxes, king of kings, who always insisted that visitors tuck their hands in their sleeves to protect himself from assassination.

Modern, three-dimensional Picasso-like rendering marks style of this statuette of a goddess.  British Museum.

chapter 13

WHY THE EMPIRE COLLAPSED

ON February 16, 423 B.C., a prominent Babylonian "banker" named Enlil-nadin-shum rented a house in Babylon for the enormous sum of a pound and a half of silver "until the going-forth of the king." Darius II had just mounted the Achaemenid throne and was visiting Babylon. Enlil-nadin-shum, head of the firm of Murashu Sons in the city of Nippur, was anxious to pay his respects. He also was eager to find out if this king, like the previous one, would support the banker's business.

For *banker,* in this case, we can substitute *loan shark.* Murashu Sons of Nippur was notorious for its outrageous rates of interest, as much as 40 percent per year, or approximately double the rate of any previous time in history. Not only did the loan sharks hold a borrower's land as collateral, but Murashu Sons worked the land for their own profit until the borrower paid back the loan—if ever he could. Since these abuses had gone on for years without royal interference, it seems likely that Murashu Sons made regular and liberal donations to the royal treasury in return for royal protection.

No wonder, then, that Enlil-nadin-shum was anxious to see the king this day, regardless of cost. A pound and a half of silver

Hunting the wild horses and capturing them with a lasso, a popular Persian sport, is depicted in this relief. British Museum.

was incredible rent, but Babylon was crowded. Alas for Enlil-nadin-shum! Babylon was crowded because the king was leaving for Susa this day. The loan shark never did obtain a royal audience. Eleven days later he was back at Nippur, making up his lost expense money by charging two poor women his usual 40 percent interest rate.

All of this we know from the Murashu archives, part of the vast collection of Babylonian tablets and documents that archaeologists have unearthed. From these sources and written histories of the time comes a vivid picture of the decline of the Achaemenid Empire. It is a sad story. It is also a familiar story. More than one great civilization has gone the way of the Achaemenids, through moral and economic decay, speeded by sheer neglect.

At the time of Xerxes' death the empire was staggering under its tax burden. Persia itself paid no taxes, but every other corner of the realm paid dearly. Media was assessed 450 talents and a

This majestic bull, sculpted from gray marble, is one of two that adorned a pillar capital in the great hall at Persepolis. Oriental Institute, University of Chicago.

tribute of 100,000 sheep. A talent then equaled approximately $1,300, although the difference in buying power between our time and then makes comparison almost meaningless. Susa paid 300 talents. Armenia paid 400 and sent the king 20,000 prized Nesaean horses every year at the time of the Mithra feast.

Some satrapies were forced to provide boys and girls for the court. The Indians of Hindush — true empire loyalists to the end (and rewarded for their loyalty and their fighting prowess by being placed next to the Immortals in guarding the king's person) — paid 360 talents of gold dust a year, the tribute highest in actual value. Libya and Egypt together gave up 700 talents, plus profits from their fisheries, plus 120,000 measures of grain to feed the local Persian garrison. Arabia contributed 1,000 talents worth of frankincense. Every three years Ethiopia sent gold, ebony, elephant tusks, and boys.

Miserable Babylonia, harshly punished for her frequent revolts, paid the empire's highest silver tax, 1,000 talents, and a humiliating gift of 500 boys to be made eunuchs.  Also, because Babylonia was close to Susa and had fertile land, it fed the court four months of every year.  Many Babylonians dedicated their daughters to be courtesans when they grew up; it was the only way they could escape the degrading poverty, if not outright starvation, of home.

This annual torrent of gold, silver, and goods then amounted to some 14,560 talents, about $20 million, with a purchasing power many times larger than the sum suggests.  Such was the king of king's private income for his court, armies, and treasury.

Molten gold and silver were poured into jars to harden.  Some of the bullion was stored, some was made into coins.  By 465 B.C. the empire was being drained of precious metals, and their use declined.  Business continued with the use of credit, but the demand for actual silver in payment of taxes persisted.  Soon loan sharks and the court held the bulk of the coinage.  Most of the officials, landowners, and judges were Persians.  Inflation increased, prices soared beyond all reason, and everywhere non-Persians suffered.

The killing of Xerxes in 465 touched off 130 years of sickening violence.  Murders occurred with monotonous regularity. Xerxes' eighteen-year-old son, Artaxerxes, murdered two of his brothers, plus several other men who blocked his way to the throne.

At times this particular king seemed totally unreasonable. During a hunt one day a lion charged Artaxerxes.  A courtier speared the beast, saving the king's life.  The courtier's reward was a death sentence, because the law forbade the killing of an animal in the presence of the king.  Luckily, others at court pleaded for his life and the courtier was merely banished.

When Artaxerxes himself passed on in 424 (one of the few of his family to die of natural causes), his son Xerxes II took the throne.  Forty-five days later he was assassinated by his half brother Secydianus, while sleeping off a drunken party.  Secydianus was in turn murdered by still another half brother, who

then became King Darius II.  He started his reign by having
a courtier stoned to death (for burying Xerxes II without royal
consent).  He subsequently murdered several others who stood
in his path and occupied the uneasy throne for nineteen years,
strongly influenced by his wife, Parysatis, who was also his half
sister, and who proved to be even more ruthless than he.

Undoubtedly some of the royal sickness was related to generations of incestuous marriages such as this one.  Then, too,
ambitious court eunuchs were forever scheming and making
trouble behind the scenes.

Darius II finally died, never once having led his troops into
battle.  But the procession of murderous kings and princes went
on and on.  The Persian army, lacking a competent leader,
became a laughingstock throughout the empire.

Only Persian money was respected.  A coin of the time bore
the replica of a Persian archer; a favorite joke among the satraps
went, "The Persian archer can do what the Persian spearman can-
not."  A constant flow of bribes kept enemies appeased or pitted
against one another.  Only bribery prevented Greece from
capitalizing on its early victories:  Persian money set the Athenians and Spartans at each other's throats, touching off the thirty-
year Peloponnesian War.

Even bribery sometimes failed to work.  Egypt rebelled and
the king seemed powerless to recover it.  Sparta was belligerent
and gaining strength.  Several satraps revolted against the
burden of taxation, formed a coalition, and issued their own
coinage.  This was the supreme insult to the king of kings.
Somehow Darius II's successor, Artaxerxes II, held on for nearly
fifty years, though the empire was literally falling apart.

The reign of Artaxerxes II was most noteworthy for yet another
Persian military and moral defeat and another glorious page in
Grecian history.  Although Artaxerxes was the oldest son and
logical successor to his father's throne, Queen Parysatis had her
own favorite, a son named Cyrus.  She urged Cyrus to murder his
brother while the latter was getting into his coronation robes.

Cyrus was caught preparing to do exactly that.  Queen Parysatis began wailing and pleading so effectively that the new king let his treacherous brother go free.  He even gave him back his job, heading one of the satrapies.

That moment of compassion nearly cost Artaxerxes II his throne and his life.  Within three years young Cyrus was back leading his own troops, plus 13,000 Greek mercenaries.  The Greek *hoplites* (heavy-armed foot soldiers) and *peltasts* (light-armed foot soldiers) were the world's finest infantrymen.  When they clashed with Artaxerxes' army on September 3, 401, they routed part of the Persian force.  Then impetuous Cyrus rushed at his brother and wounded him, but was himself slain with a javelin.  By now Artaxerxes II lost all traces of brotherly love.  He ordered Cyrus' head and hand paraded around as proof of his death and a warning to other traitors.

Ten thousand of the Greek mercenaries meanwhile stood leaderless but intact.  Artaxerxes shrank from attacking this formidable force.  Then, in a remarkable show of Greek democracy and courage, the Greek troops elected new leaders and set out on a seven-hundred-mile homeward march through the heart of the Achaemenid Empire.  This incredible feat, which became a Greek classic, further shattered the Achaemenids' reputation.

By 358 one of Artaxerxes' sons, a cold-blooded character named Ochus, survived a round of palace murders to emerge as King Artaxerxes III.  He was a sour-faced man with a short, straight nose, short hair, and a long, pointed beard.  His first official act was to murder all his relatives, regardless of age or sex.  The number ran to several dozen.  Having disposed of local opposition, he turned to the satrapies.  He crushed the rebellious Caducians, warned Greece to behave, and recaptured Egypt.  Its pharaoh fled, its cities were ravaged, its temples were plundered.  Not since Darius had the empire been so strong.  Perhaps it would recover its lands.

By this time, however, a new force was emerging in the world: Macedonia, a land of vigorous people, not of Greek descent but much influenced by Greek culture.    Since 360, Philip, the Macedonian king, had expanded his influence and holdings in the Grecian world and had kept his eye on Asia.    He also had a brilliant, ambitious son named Alexander.    Together in 338 B.C. they conquered Greece.

That same year Artaxerxes was poisoned by his doctor on orders from the eunuch Bagoas.    His son Arses held the throne for two years, but he antagonized the eunuch kingmaker and also was poisoned.    The successor, Darius III, nearly joined the casualty list, but he discovered the plot against his life and forced Bagoas to swallow the deadly drink that had been prepared for him.

Darius III showed signs of strength.    Given a chance, he might have salvaged something from the ruins.    But it was too late. The empire was a hollow shell, ready to be crushed by any outside force.

And that force was at hand, in the person of the greatest conqueror of them all.

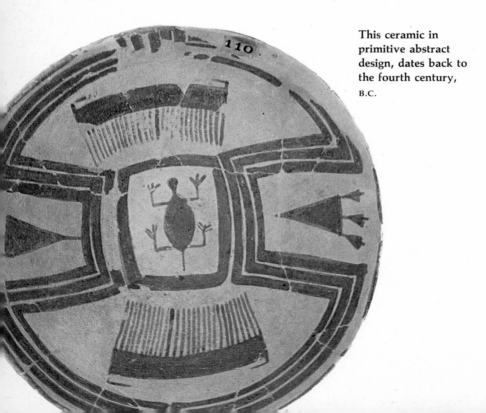

This ceramic in primitive abstract design, dates back to the fourth century, B.C.

chapter 14

SUPERMAN FROM MACEDONIA

Even if the Persian Empire had remained as mighty as it was in its finest hours, Alexander the Great very likely would have toppled it. From the day he was born, in 356 B.C., to the day he died, in 323, Alexander had style. While others plodded through life, this remarkable man seemed to leap from peak to peak.

He had the qualities that men admire and that made men heroes in his day: strength, good looks, a talent for leadership, courage in battle, a modicum of humanity in peace, and a grasp of ideas beyond the reach of lesser mortals. A supreme opportunist, Alexander could be ruthless. But he was nevertheless "great," not because he was always admirable, but because he dominated the world of his time.

Alexander was trained in the manly arts by a Greek named Leonidas, who evidently gloried in memories of his Spartan namesake. He toughened the boy with such meager meals and exhausting all-night marches that his mother, taking pity on him, used to smuggle him snacks. From age thirteen to sixteen Alexander's tutor was Aristotle, the Greek philosopher, surely the finest teacher in all antiquity. Among other things, he

This pair of bronze horses project the verve and dash of the teams that drew the famed Assyrian chariots, suggests that they may be the creations of Assyrian artisans. Oriental Institute, University of Chicago.

trained the boy in logical thinking. Alexander learned his lessons well. He grew into manhood not tall but seeming so, erect and athletic, with curly fair hair, long, straight nose, clean-shaven face.

Alexander was fiercely ambitious. Visitors from far-off Persia found the prince uncommonly interested in their land. At sixteen, serving as regent of Macedonia while his father was off to the wars, he seized the chance to defeat some neighboring barbarian tribes and to found a new city, Alexandropolis.

When an enemy stabbed Philip to death at a wedding ceremony, in 336, Alexander probably wasted little time in grief. For one thing, he was too busy. He disposed of other pretenders to the throne promptly and bloodily, with his mother's help. At twenty he was king.

Immediately he set his sights on Persia, not only in his role as King of Macedonia, but as commander in chief of the Corinth League and avenger of the Grecian states. First he had to secure his home base and his flanks, by raids to the north and west.

From the beginning he showed a genius for war, an unerring instinct for when and how to attack. He could adapt to any

How Persian pomp and power must have looked to a Greek is portrayed in
a detail from this Greek vase. Here a satrap stands before a Persian king
to give an accounting of himself. He is standing on base of gold, the weight
of which will vary, according to how much the king believes of what he is
saying. National Archaeological Museum of Italy, Naples.

situation. One tribal enemy loosed an avalanche of wagons
downhill on the Macedonians. Alexander had anticipated the
trick and briefed his troops. Those who could darted aside to
let the wagons pass. Others lay flat with their shields interlocked

over their heads, probably aided by buffers of stones or shallow earth-embankments, and let the wagons bounce harmlessly over or around them.  Again, the young king made a surprise crossing of a river—and subsequently won a battle—by having his men turn their animalskin tents into hay-stuffed tied-up floats, which they rode across the stream.  This was a tactic he used often in later campaigns.

Alexander inherited from his father one of the best military machines in the ancient world, and he improved upon it.  The enemies of Macedonia, including the Persians, were fighting much as their forefathers had.  Alexander improvised.

The phalanx and the cavalry made up the main segments of his army.  The phalanx consisted of 9,000 foot soldiers in units of 256—16 men square.  These phalangites were superbly trained and disciplined.  They kept a distance of three feet between men, so that a sudden enemy onslaught or a charge over rough ground would not send them tumbling over each other.  The phalanx could shift from rectangular to square formation on command. Indeed, this was only one of its tricks.  Alexander sometimes used drill squad routines as a sort of psychological warfare before the actual battle.  These gymnastics so awed some of his enemies that they took to their heels.

At the right of the phalanx rode Alexander in gleaming helmet crowned with crest and white plumes, wielding a sword of specially tempered steel.  He led the crack Royal Squadron, part of his two-thousand-man Companion Cavalry—heavily armored riders with short swords and short spears.  Another squadron rode on the left wing.

His cavalry tactics were almost as dazzling as the phalangite footwork.  Alexander held back his horsemen until a break showed in the enemy line.  Then he charged his right wing Royal Squadron into the weak spot.  Why just the right wing riders? Alexander had reasoned it out:  Most foot soldiers carried shields in the left hand, swords in the right.  There was a natural tendency in the line of battle to drift to one's right, for the additional protection of a neighbor's shield.  By riding on the right side of his own men, Alexander lessened their tendency to stray. By making his first cavalry charge to the enemy's left, he increased their natural drift to the right. And as he pushed them in that direction, his left wing cavalry closed in to complete the slaughter. It worked with incredible regularity.

All told, Alexander marched with about 30,000 infantry and 5,000 cavalry, plus cooks, baggage attendants, signalers with trumpets and flags, siege towers on wheels, hundred-foot battering rams, machines for tunneling under enemy walls, and huge catapults.

In the year 334 B.C. Alexander led this war machine on his great march—a march of eleven years and thousands of miles, from which he would never return. Professional historians assembled, and perhaps inflated, the events into a full-fledged chronicle. The king also took along surveyors, botanists, and geographers, for he was no ordinary ravaging-conqueror. He saw his march as a great adventure, an expansion of man's knowledge, a probing of the mysterious outer world, which he assumed would end at a mighty sea somewhere beyond Persia.

His first confrontation with the Persians took place in May of that year at the Granicus River, near the southwest corner of the Black Sea. A sizable Persian force, led by the local satrap, was waiting across the river.

The battle raged around Alexander. A javelin pierced the joint in his breastplate. Two Persian generals rushed at him. He broke his spear on one and went for his sword. He reeled from a battle-ax blow that nearly demolished his helmet. Then just as one of the Persians was about to decapitate him from behind, a boyhood friend named Cleitus cut down that man while Alexander finished the other. When the Macedonians charged with new ferocity, the Persians broke. The battle was over. Alexander ordered most of the Greek mercenaries on the Persian side slaughtered and the rest sent home in chains—an object lesson for traitors to the League of Corinth.

Yet Alexander promptly followed this harsh treatment of the

enemy with the kind of gesture that helped him keep his men, despite hardship and minor mutinies, year after year, mile after weary mile, far away from home.  On this occasion he buried the dead and ordered that their parents and children be exempt from taxes.  He visited his wounded, listened to their bragging, and complimented them.  That autumn he sent the newly married soldiers home to their wives for the winter.  His men, for the most part, idolized him, and no wonder.

In October of 333 Darius and Alexander met face to face at Issus, about midway between Jerusalem and the Black Sea. The Persians outnumbered the Greeks, but not by many, and the battle went exactly as Alexander wanted it:  phalangite thrust, crack in the enemy line, quick cavalry charge into the enemy center.  And suddenly there, looming from his chariot in the middle of the Persian horde (where he always traveled), was Darius III, last king of kings.

The fighting closed around him.  His nobles, relatives, and Immortals formed a human shield and died like flies.  Alexander himself took a sword thrust in the right thigh.  Then Darius' horses, peppered with spears and mad with fright and pain, reared and threatened to upset him.  Suddenly Darius wheeled and fled, leaving his mother, wife, and two daughters in camp and his army in shambles.

Alexander lingered to help finish the Greek mercenaries attached to the Persian army, who were putting up their usual splendid fight, then pursued the runaway until night.  At one point, his scribes recorded, Alexander crossed a gully filled with the bodies of slaughtered men.  Darius lost his chariot, bow, shield, and mantle and had to take to horseback — but he escaped.

Alexander returned to the Persian camp to taste the first real luxuries of conquest.  He bathed in Darius' tub, marveled at pitchers and caskets of gold, passed through tents fragrant with spices, and finally sat down to a sumptuous banquet in the loser's tent.  "This, it seems, is to be a king!" he told his friends.

Would Alexander content himself with half the Persian

Empire? Or would he pursue and destroy Darius immediately? Neither. The young king now veered toward Egypt, taking one coastal city after another until he came to the island city of Tyre.

Alexander pecked away at Tyre for seven months, building a causeway to the walls and bringing in a newly captured navy to assist him. The defenders rolled boulders into the sea to hold off Macedonian ships, tangled the enemy in nets as they tried to scale the walls, dumped scorching hot sand that got inside enemy armor, lowered sharp hooks on long poles to sever the ropes that controlled Macedonian battering rams.

Finally, Alexander broke into the city, murdered about eight thousand defenders, and angrily sold the other thirty thousand into slavery.

On he forged, seemingly unbeatable, sweeping the world before him only four years after ascending the throne. He took the Arabs of Gaza, suffering a shoulder wound from a catapult in the process. Egypt gave up without a struggle, being sick of Persian rule, and Alexander designated himself pharaoh—literally, a son of the Egyptian god.

Whether he realized it or not, Alexander was adopting certain tactics that had made the Achaemenids great—restoring to captive peoples an element of self-government, posing at times as friend, admirer of local customs, and logical successor to local thrones.

He turned east again. Once more he caught up with Darius, on October 1, 331, across the Tigris River, near the town of Guagamela. The king of kings planned an all-out fight. His cavalry was still as good as any in the world. He was short of infantry, but he had a few surprises. His men were prepared to sprinkle the battle plain with caltrops—four-pronged pieces of metal, containing three prongs which would lodge in the ground, leaving the fourth upraised to spike the hooves of charging horses. He built scythe chariots, with a long, sharp pole protruding between the horses in front and blades attached to the wheels at the sides. He brought up fifteen elephants to panic enemy horses and crunch the enemy infantry.

Again the numbers were nearly even, with a slight edge for Persia.  As the battle began, Alexander deliberately led his troops to the right.  Darius realized that his scythe chariots would be drawn away from the level ground he had cleared for them.  He ordered the chariot charge.  But this time the Macedonian phalanx was fronted with javelin-throwers, stone-slingers, and archers.  They crippled or killed many horses and drivers.  As the remaining chariots charged, the phalanx parted to let them and their vicious whirling blades pass through.  Then it was easy to jump them from behind.

Back at the front line it was a familiar story: phalanx pounding Persian infantry until a gap showed in the Persian line and the Companion Cavalry charged.  Alexander had ordered his men to strike at Persian faces—a particularly unnerving tactic.  A virile young soldier didn't mind a body wound, but the thought of going home with a mutilated face terrified him.  The Mace-

Another representation of a Persian king done in relief on the palace walls at Susa.  British Museum.

donians again pushed in close to Darius.  For a second time the king of kings had to run.  Again Alexander paused, to help his left wing cavalry, and Darius again escaped after an all-day chase. But the end was near.

Alexander marched to Babylon, which surrendered without a fight.  In return he treated the people well, appointed a local satrap (aided by Macedonian military and financial officers), and rebuilt the temple that Xerxes had dragged down long ago, taking part in Babylonian religious rites.

He then took Susa, richest prize of all.  Here the Persian kings had hidden away some fifty thousand talents in gold and silver. Alexander appropriated it for Macedonia and moved to Persepolis in 330.  This symbol of the Persian empire was his, with its countless ornamental treasures and its quarter billion dollars worth of gold.  He might have kept most of the money himself, for he was almost without personal funds, but he fed the fortune back into his own new empire and stimulated a political and economic boom.

Then, incongruously, Alexander committed his most wanton and senseless act, the burning of Persepolis.  Some historians think it was an accident, but most believe it was a deliberate message to the world from Alexander the Great: See how I have crushed the Persian Empire.  (He actually may have done historians a favor; the fire baked hundreds of clay tablets that would otherwise have crumbled centuries before archaeologists found them.)

A little later and farther east he would find the body of Darius. The Persian king had been stabbed by rebels in his own ranks. Alexander would march on into India, obstinately, alienating old friends with his singlemindedness, driven by his thirst for power and his growing pride.  For seven more years he would march, only to die at thirty-three, worn out by wounds and too many campaigns.  But all of this was anticlimactic for the Persian Empire.  Its final chapter was written in the smoke from Persepolis.  The Achaemenids had gone.

chapter 15

THE LEGACY

$W_{AS}$ the empire dead?
In one sense, yes.   The Achaemenids were gone forever.   In another sense, no.   Their empire left an indelible impression on the world.

In some ways the mark is quite clear.   The Medes and Persians allowed a radical new religion to rise in their midst.   It fostered a more ethical kind of human conduct, and it has reached down through the ages into some of our religions today.   The Achaemenids created a distinct and grandiose form of art.   They permitted widespread use of a language (Aramaic) not their own. They invented the pony-express system of speedily relaying messages by road.   They fostered a moderate amount of science: Under Darius III, for example, a Babylonian astronomer named Naburimanni studied lunar eclipses and made calculations more accurate than those of either Ptolemy or Copernicus, who followed him.

Perhaps the greatest tangible achievement of the Achaemenids is modern Iran itself.   The generations who followed the Medes and Persians, like their ancestors, are people of amazing vitality. Time after time, in the centuries after Alexander the Great, that

one-time land of the Achaemenids—the strategic land-link between East and West, always coveted by conquerors—has been
swept by mankind's fiercest invaders.    Among them were
Parthians, Turks, Mongols, Arabs fired with religious zeal, and
well-drilled legions from Rome.    Somehow the Persians absorbed
all of them and with them their cultures; yet they continued to
maintain a distinct Persian character.    So, today, the people
of Iran claim, with much validity, that the Persian monarchy,

Luristan bronze of horse
and trainer had been
stolen from a tomb like
many others.  It was
found only recently
among the ordinary
objects in the Hamadan
bazaars.  Louvre.

Design similar to that later used in Persian carpets was chiselled in stone to ornament the walls of the great hall in the palace at Persepolis. British Museum.

having stayed alive for twenty-five hundred continuous years, is the oldest political institution in the world.

The Greek rule that followed Alexander's death ended in the second century B.C., when the Parthians, an Iranian tribe from the north, revolted. They in turn were ousted in A.D. 226 by the Sassanians from the province of Fars. Under the Sassanians, who claimed Achaemenid ancestry, the old Persian style in art, in government, and in religion came back. This period contributed other elements to the world: chess, for example, which Persians found in India and relayed to the West; and polo, which may have been born in the northern steppes but was developed under the Sassanians.

In the thirteen centuries since the Sassanians were defeated by the Arabs, Persia—now Iran—has enjoyed true political independence for a total of only about four hundred years.  Yet always those descendants of the Achaemenids managed to produce things of value under their various masters and to share those things with the world.

They created exquisite miniature paintings, for instance, a unique art-form that flourished from the fifteenth to the seventeenth centuries.  The strangely flat, primitive human figures in these tiny pictures stem from the earliest Achaemenid art.  But the miniatures were made in this way to get around an Islamic ban on reproducing the human figure; and they were made small deliberately, so that they could be quickly hidden among the pages of a book.

Fine carpets, another product of Persia, originally intended to be hung on the wall not spread on the floor, reflect that Achaemenid talent for decoration.  Even words have come down to us through the ages, and give color to our language today.  More than one hundred fifty English words are derived from Persian:  such words as bazaar, naptha, sherbet, pajama, orange, margarine, khaki, sugar.  In such unrecognized ways the lively ghosts of the Achaemenids still walk among us.

There is yet another legacy, intangible but important.  In this world there will always be some who rule and many who are ruled.  The Achaemenids lifted the function of ruling to a fine art.  They showed that tyranny could successfully practice creative management.  By allowing their subject peoples to keep their faith, their customs, their private gods and beloved rituals, the best of those conquerors kept the people relatively content.  The empire remained cohesive and prosperous.  And so, twenty-four centuries ago, the Medes and Persians offered a preview of the future:  a possibility that many nationalities can live together and maintain their individual identity.

# Suggested Reading

In addition to the major sources cited below, I am indebted to the Bible, Encyclopedia Britannica and Dr. T. Cuyler Young, Jr., of the Royal Ontario Museum. To Cuyler Young, in particular, for access to his own writing, to the Royal Ontario Museum artifacts, and for hours of good conversation and valuable advice, I owe much thanks.

Benveniste, Emile. *The Persian Religion According to the Chief Greek Texts.* P. Geuthner, Paris, 1929. A summary by the leading French scholar on Zoroastrianism of what we can learn of Iranian religion in the Achaemenid Period.

Bury, John B. *History of Greece.* MacMillan and Co., Ltd. London, 1920. One of the best histories of Greece, in which there is a great deal on the Achaemenids. Dated, but solid.

Cameron, George G. *History of Early Iran.* Greenwood Press, N.Y., 1968. One of the few books in English that deal with the Medes.

Frye, Richard. *The Heritage of Persia.* Weidenfeld and Nicolson, London, 1962. A scholarly book concerned with the problem of Iranian cultural roots.

Herodotus. *The Histories.* G. P. Putnam's Sons, N.Y., 1960. A major source on the period; full of good storytelling.

Kent, Roland G. *Old Persian.* American Oriental Society, New Haven, 1953. The standard edition of the Old Persian inscriptions of the Achaemenid kings.

Olmstead, Albert T. E. *History of the Persian Empire.* University of Chicago Press, 1959. The standard history on the period in English, although now somewhat dated.

Porada, Edith. *The Art of Ancient Iran.* Crown, N.Y., 1965. Best semi-popular book on Iranian art available.

Xenophon. *The Persian Expedition.* Penguin Books, Harmondsworth, Middlesex, 1952. Sometimes called *The March of the Ten Thousand.* Story of the revolt of Cyrus the Younger against Artaxerxes II and the homeward trip of the Greek soldiers who fought in Cyrus' lost cause.

# Index